On Locations

On Locations

Lessons Learned from My Life On Set with
The Sopranos and in the Film Industry

MARK KAMINE

STEERFORTH PRESS
LEBANON, NEW HAMPSHIRE

For information about permission to reproduce
selections from this book, write to:
Steerforth Press, 31 Hanover Street, Suite 1
Lebanon, New Hampshire 03766

Cataloging-in-Publication Data is available from the Library of Congress

Paperback ISBN 978-1-58642-403-9

Printed in the United States of America

For Tana
and for Jack, Christine, and Daisy

Contents

I've always been anxious, fearful,
competitive, envious and angry.

— David Chase, *The New York Times*,
June 6, 1999

Foreword

Throughout my career, I've had bad experiences with line producers. It's not always their fault. They must play the role of the in-house heavy, and their job is to tell me when I've asked for too much. I can handle a "NO" (mostly), but sometimes I find the manner in which the "NO" is delivered to be unforgivable. If she defends her "NO" with only mumbo jumbo about budgets and studio mandates, I lose all trust. Does this philistine care only about the bottom line? What about art and my vision? For this sequence to work, I need 200 extras and the yacht to explode – don't you get it, you traitorous myopic weasel?

Mark Kamine came into my life, I don't exactly remember when. It was a job interview, and he seemed affable enough – he said all the right things about my script, and how his job is to support the director, yadda yadda – but I didn't trust him – because I'm a junkyard dog and I wasn't born yesterday, and line producers are shady as hell. I got home and began my due diligence with a Google search, and to my confusion, up came a bunch of inarguably well-written book reviews. A line producer who is also an astute reader of literature – and a great writer himself? This can't be the same Mark Kamine. But it was. I haven't worked with another line producer since.

Mark and I have shared some amazing experiences in the past few years. Maui at sunset, drinking cocktails – made by his wife, Tana – the only guests of a giant, fully-staffed hotel. Dinners in Sicily, watching Mount Etna shoot red lava into the night sky. Location scouts that extended into "atmospheric pilgrimages," touring some of the most picturesque spots in Japan, Thailand, and France. We have shared moments of pain, too – crazy long hours, insufferable actors, angry network calls. But even in the darkest moments, I have never lost my trust in Mark. It really does help to have a fellow writer minding the store. When he says "NO," I sense it pains him more than it does me. I still go back to my hotel room cursing his name, but it takes the edge off.

It's not just with me – Mark engages *everyone* with a writer's curiosity and respect. He knows we are all heroes in our own stories – and, therefore, treads lightly and kindly as he goes about his job, careful not to become someone else's villain. I love him for that – and this reminds me of my one quibble with this book. In it, he says the showrunner – and perhaps a few of the actors – are crucial to the creative enterprise. Everyone else, including him, is replaceable. I disagree. Not to get too airy-fairy, but I believe that the art reflects the collaborative, alchemical spirit in which it is made. Mark is a leader of our show, and his humanist outlook – born of his writerly mind – is essential to the final product, and I am grateful for it.

There is one downside to having a writer in his position – a creeping suspicion that Mark is taking notes and will one day bear witness to all that he's seen. After reading this great memoir, I have a right to be paranoid. When I'm an asshole – or an idiot – or a pretentious artiste who demands 200 extras and an exploding yacht, I can now assume it will all be revealed in the follow-up to *On Locations*. But it's a price I'm happily willing to pay.

Mike White
Thailand
April 2023

My New Jersey Family, Part One

My father's wife, Grace, calls me about my father. This is a few years before I meet my wife, Tana, before I go to film school, before I start working in the biz, but after I've come through the severest period of anxiety attacks and agoraphobia that hit me in my early twenties. It's 1986. The conversation below, as with all the conversations in this book, is an approximation, some of it clear in my mind, some the result of a conviction of proper pace and meaning, some simply my best guess.

After we say hello, Grace asks, "Do you think you could come out and talk to your father?"

I am surprised and to some extent put on guard by this. We aren't estranged by any means. I get invited to occasional sporting events and dinners and, more regularly, holiday parties. But clearly this isn't that. We don't have a stop-by-without-occasion relationship. I've never been asked to come over to, simply, talk. In truth we don't, my father and I, in any substantive way, talk.

"What's up?" I say.

"He's having a hard time."

"Meaning . . . ?"

"Well, he's not getting out of bed."

It sounds like she's talking about a kid sick with the flu, not my father, longtime forceful, often silent, and usually serious straight shooter who came up on the working-class east side of Paterson, New Jersey, went from there to college, to Korea, back to college then on to law school, and now lives on top of a desirable hill in Wayne, the suburb west of Paterson where I grew up. He was a distant and sometimes strict parent with a solo law practice, played catcher on a scarily intense adult fast-pitch softball team, and drove indefatigably anytime we went anywhere. He hasn't, in my awareness, changed much. I don't know what to make of what I'm being told. I assume that my recent experience with anxiety and analysis bears on my being asked to come talk to him. It makes me the family expert on — on what? Sudden descent? Incapacity? The options for treatment if you can't figure out how to get yourself out of bed?

"How long has it been?" I ask.

"Two weeks," she says.

"Wow."

"Yeah."

"Anyone have any idea what it's about?"

"I sure don't," she says. "He doesn't seem to."

"Got it," I say. "I'll come by. I'll try to get there tomorrow. I'll get there tomorrow. I'll let you know when."

"Tomorrow would be good."

I borrow a friend's car and drive out. Grace opens the door almost instantly. She thanks me for coming and waves a hand in the air, indicating upstairs. "In bed like I said," she says. Then she says, "Archie! Mark's here!"

She nods me up.

And there he is, lying flat on his back on the big, canopied bed, head elevated by a couple of pillows, eyes wide and unblinking.

"Hey, Dad," I say. "What's going on?"

He says nothing, looks at me with the wide eyes.

"You want to talk about it?" I ask. "Grace said you're having trouble getting out of bed."

"I don't know what's wrong with me," he says.

"There's nothing physically wrong? Is that what you mean?"

He nods. "I don't . . . I can't get up," he says.

"Okay, you're, you're not feeling good. It feels, what, like you're weak" – I am watching him closely, and he gives the slightest shake of his head – "or maybe more like it's pointless?"

This conversation is going slowly. This is the way it happened: Him in his bed, under the covers, head propped up. Me standing at the end of the bed looking down at him. I have rarely been in their bedroom. The first time was when they gave me the tour after they first moved in, rightfully proud. It's a beautiful house. A big, beautiful bedroom, big windows looking out over trees and a distant lake, a spacious bathroom through an area of walk-in closets.

"Like there's no point to . . . anything?" I say.

No response.

"Grace said it's been a couple weeks," I then say.

"Yeah," he says.

"Did anything happen a couple weeks ago? What happened recently?"

"Nothing, really," he says. "I put forty grand down on an office condo on the Turnpike. To move the office to."

He has been renting three rooms in a low-rise office building in a strip mall parking lot a few miles from his house. The first time I saw the strip mall space, which by this time he's been working in for several years, I was crestfallen. The rooms were small. His secretary mostly worked at his big desk in the main office, and he spent his time at the short conference table in what he called the library, where I built him a wall of dark-wood bookshelves to lend the place a legal flavor. I was not a great carpenter. I did all right with the shelves, but the office had a cramped, fluorescent-lit, cheaply constructed feel, and the shelves loomed over the conference table with threatening weight. When I saw what they looked like – dangerous – I attached numerous angle irons to the underside of every other shelf to anchor the structure to the wall. His prior office in Paterson, before his move to the strip mall, had been in a grandish Federal-style building, smoked glass with his name in black letters on the entrance door, big rooms with marble columns half sunk into the retrofitted plaster walls, big windows looking out at a real city. The strip mall office looked across a parking lot to Wayne Valley High School. I couldn't blame him for wanting something nicer.

"And now you don't want to move the office there?" I ask.

"I signed a contract," he says. "I mean what if I . . . what if I can't work? I used Nicole's college savings for it."

Nicole is my half-sister, twenty years younger than me.

"Maybe you can get out of it."

"I signed the contract."

"You could ask, though. People understand."

"I could ask."

He doesn't seem sure about it. He's looking at me.

"Can't hurt," I say.

"No," he says.

"So," I say. "So, what do you think's going on?"

"I think Grace is gonna leave me if this keeps up is what I think," he says. "I mean, how much of this will she put up with?"

"I don't think she's leaving you. More like she's concerned about you."

"I mean, what's wrong with me? It's pathetic."

"Well, as you know with what happened to me, these things happen. I mean you took me to the doctor those first couple of times I had panic attacks. And I couldn't leave the house for a while. Like, I got panicky anytime I went anywhere."

"Yeah, you weren't in good shape."

"The therapy helps," I say. "Talking. I mean the Valiums didn't hurt, either."

"I don't think I can do therapy," he says.

"No?"

"It's not me," he says.

I resist the obvious, *This isn't you, either*. Instead, I say, "Okay. But maybe you should talk to someone. I mean a friend. What about, I don't know, John would be a good person to talk to I bet. He's seen tons of this, I'm sure. Actors, right?" I smile.

My father lies there, eyes on me.

John is married to my father's wife's sister. He was in an experimental theater company in the 1960s and early 1970s, performing at La Ma Ma and other downtown theater spaces. Their plays had lots of energy, profanity, bawdiness. At some point John's company hooked up with the Public Theater, where they performed their own stuff and whatever came along. Their regular director started mentoring John and eventually handed his baton over on one of their bigger shows, a Broadway revival of *The Pirates of Penzance*. Now John is directing plays and is starting to get into three-camera TV, soaps and sit-coms. My father loves being a sometime part of his world, and in return invites John to his club. They play tennis, have drinks and dinner. John is easy to talk to.

"I could," he says.

"Sure," I say. "Call him. Talk about how you're feeling. Or just tell him how you don't feel like doing anything and see where it leads."

"Need to do something," he says. "She'll leave me if I don't."

"I'm sorry you're going through this, Dad," I say.

"Your grandfather had these things, I remember. A few times. He'd go into a black hole. For months sometimes."

"Really?" I say.

I'd never heard this. His father, my grandfather, is steady, healthy, active. Eighty, still sharp, drives himself all over, lives in the senior apartments not far from his son's office, still fills in at the counter at Tabatchnik's delicatessen, where he used to work.

"Like a cloud came over him," my father says.

"Runs in the family, I guess," I say.

This gets a smile from him.

"You saying we're all cracked?" he says.

This gets a smile from me.

2

Movie Star

Driving a van around Upper Manhattan, my eyes glancing in the rearview mirror at the location manager in the back or at the map on my lap, slowing down even at green lights to check the street signs, I can't bring myself to say out loud, *I am lost.* Everyone in the van is either my boss or outranks me in some way. The location manager. The production designer sitting beside him. The producer in the next row forward, directly behind me. The director of photography beside him. And above all, the director, next to me in the passenger seat. The movie is *Quiz Show*, my first job on a Hollywood feature. Between the director and me, on top of a cooler full of drinks, sits a wireless phone in a bulky bag, precursor of the cell phone. The year is 1993, before GPS maps were our guides.

The director is Robert Redford.

While I drive, lost and speechless, he looks around.

"It's amazing," he says, "that you can live in a place like New York for years, your whole life, and be not ten, fifteen minutes from your house, and not know where you are. For example, you" – he turns and addresses me – "might not know where you are now."

Each time Redford talks to someone on the phone as we drive, he'll report with seeming pride: "I'm in the van in New York scouting locations."

Before the movie got off the ground, the first time he called the office: "It's Bob, is Michael there?"

———

I was thirty-five. I had a son about to be two years old. I worked in the producer's downtown Manhattan office. I was not getting paid. It was for the experience.

"If one of these projects gets off the ground, I'll stick you in locations," the producer told me. "They'll have the biggest department early on."

When I told my wife I got a job with a producer she was excited until I added I wouldn't be getting paid. She then expressed her displeasure. I couldn't blame her. We'd been married three and a half years, together for five. A few months after we met, I got into and decided to go to film school, which I began the following fall. Three years and $30,000 in loans later, I was working for free.

I temped at corporations the days the producer didn't need me. Once when I asked an administrative assistant I was working alongside what the symbol for multiplication was in Excel since the x I'd used wasn't working, I got a look. The assistant then walked into his boss's office. The boss instantly emerged and approached. He was younger than me, and toweringly tall.

"Your profile said you knew Word and Excel," he said, "which is all we required."

He said this in the harsh voice of corporate authority. I'd heard it before on these jobs, though never directed at me. Then he leaned over and placed his hands on my temporary keyboard, changed the x in my formula to an asterisk, and walked away.

For the producer I entered data, answered phones, read scripts, and, if asked, offered my thoughts. I picked up office supplies and lunch. A few months in, I was told that Buena Vista, a Disney subsidiary, had greenlit the movie the producer had been keenest on. True to his word, he said whatever he said to the location manager, and I had a job. I'd make $400 a week, another $125 for my car.

I started by driving the production designer around the city, often weaving up and down the residential blocks of Queens and Brooklyn and slowing when the designer asked so he could record an address. He designed Redford's last movie, *A River Runs Through It*. The set designer is his girlfriend. Jodie Foster is a friend. They went to Yale together.

A team of scouts started work. When not driving the designer around, I was sent out to scout, too. I dropped off solicitation letters, followed leads, knocked on promising-looking doors, or entered period-appropriate businesses (the story was set in the late 1950s). I stopped at pay phones to call the office when paged. It was usually the assistant manager sending me to a catering hall or private club or restaurant or somewhere that someone (often the designer) wanted checked out. When I got into a potential location, I'd take photos, holding the camera sideways and snapping overlapping shots to create a panoramic view (a *pan*). I'd go to a lab on Carmine Street and wait around for the rolls to develop, meeting up with the scouts on the movie and, over the course of the next couple months, the wider group of New York scouts, who all used this lab whose owners had built their business around scouting. I'd sit on a stool at one of the counters there, taping together manila folders to make up one booklet for each location, taping my pans together and with double-stick tape pressing them into the folder (the lab would sell you boxes of folders and rolls of Scotch and double-stick tape if your office hadn't given you a supply). The scouts looked over my shoulder to offer advice. Change your F-stop rather than using the flash. Switch to a wider lens in such a small apartment. Take a cool shot to put on the cover as an enticement.

Back at the office the designer would look through everyone's folders during group sessions. The location manager,
assistant manager, and scouts circled around, making
comments as he turned the pages, a kind of hazing.

Why did you even bother? What's down this hall? You didn't
think maybe about opening this door so I could see in here?

Or (handing the folder across to the assistant manager),
Bury this deep in the trash, please.

And often, about my folders: Mark, Mark, okay, rookie
mistake. Don't do it again.

But when something good came under his gaze, he'd let
everyone know it. He'd flip back to the front of the folder

where whoever shot it had written the address, the owner's contact number, and their own name.

Barvin, nice.

Oh Robin, I love you today.

Bart does it again.

And one day: "Look at this, look at Kamine. This could work. We should see this tomorrow."

I felt proud. The process was comradely but also competitive. A couple of the other scouts gave me a look, rookie that I was – or I imagined they did.

On the first director scout, after I wait half an hour on the street beside 30 Rock, where Redford's company has its New York office, Redford gets in with the producer and we're ready to go. I clock that he sits down and doesn't fasten his seat belt. I unclip mine, pull it wide as if it's too tight, and re-click it. He doesn't get the message. He's already mid-story and keeps talking.

I am driving because the teamsters haven't started yet. The production can start them as early as it likes, but somewhere up the chain of command a decision was made to delay their start. It saves money. And since I've been driving the designer around for weeks and am not of much use as a scout, I am given the job.

Making our way down West Street to the Holland Tunnel, maybe due to nerves or the sudden stop of the car in front of me or my inexperience dealing with the fifteen-passenger van, I hit the brakes hard rather than easing to a stop.

"Mark," the producer, leaning forward, says, "careful. Precious cargo."

Another day. Driving through the narrow canyons of Wall Street, I clip the passenger-side mirror, which folds shut, and this time Redford startles.

"You'll never be a teamster, Mark," the producer says.

———

My wife, Tana, and I live in a floor-through on 15th Street between Sixth and Seventh Avenues, directly across the street from Susan Sarandon and Tim Robbins, who have a young son called Jack, like ours. We spot them now and then. Robbins is under consideration for a role in the movie, but for some reason it doesn't work out.

It's a shame, I remember thinking, cravenly. Maybe an acquaintanceship of some sort would've come from it. At this point in my career, I know nothing.

What would have been the living room of our apartment was my wife's office, two drafting tables, a desk for paperwork, shelves full of art books, flat files full of her past work. A sofa and chairs were grouped at the far end serving as a daytime conference area and nighttime living room. Under the loft storage space at the back of the room was my desk and beside it a bookcase with the small number of books I'd clung to as I moved around over the years. Tana had a successful graphic design business, corporate clients, a rotating crop of assistants fresh out of art school. One of them had a funny name, not a lot of talent, and left quickly. One was lovely, kind, and skilled. She stayed awhile then got a job as an assistant at a magazine. Then there was a guy, maybe the most talented of all but awkward, inward, and lacking a sense of hygiene and even proprioception. One summer day he came in with dirty hair and scruffy backpack as usual and, Tana later told me, got himself settled and seated, a tear in his shorts and no underwear on, his cock shifting into view each time he turned back to his drafting table or when he walked back from the bathroom or kitchen beyond the door that separated the two areas of the apartment. She carefully avoided looking at him for the rest of the day. She avoided looking at him in general. He lasted longer than she would've liked. She was distressed and relieved when he finally got another job.

We had a nanny and sometimes a babysitter for weekend nights out.

My father would not hold our baby. He was never touchy with his own children. He never, in my memory, told his children he loved them. He didn't hug, ever. I quickly became at ease with our infant son, as I was home a lot during his first two years. This was before *Quiz Show*, during film school, my classes taking up only fifteen hours a week. I had become a bit of a clean freak and had no hesitation changing Jack's diapers, cleaning his behind with baby wipes and neatly tucking him into the fresh diaper. I performed the middle-of-the-night feeding, taking the refrigerated breast milk out at 2:00 or 3:00 or 4:00 AM and lifting our son out of the crib and sitting with him in the chair in the small second bedroom as he drank up.

When I was told by Tana's father that he admired my fathering skills, I said lightly that my own father was the perfect teacher. I would only think about what he did or imagine what he would have done in a similar situation and do the opposite.

I laughed a little when I said this. But I meant it.

When the location manager and the designer pre-scout locations in prep for director scouts, I drive. They are big men. Ours is a small car, a VW Golf my wife and I bought with cash from our wedding. The designer sits up front, pushing the seat back as far as it will go, and the location manager sits sideways in back, his legs stretched across the center console, a remark about the size of the car made each time he gets in.

Early in the process we are making our way down to the Brooklyn Battery Tunnel on West Street when we see a dense white plume of smoke up ahead. The smoke, apparently emanating from beneath the sidewalk at One World Trade, climbs and widens as we approach and then pass by.

A fire or something, someone says.

Or, That doesn't look good.

Or, What the fuck?

About mid-tunnel, we see the first police cars speeding into Manhattan and, before we come out the other end, fire trucks doing the same, sirens roaring. It's February 26, 1993, sometime after 12:17 PM, and what we have scooted past I will later learn is the immediate aftermath of the detonation of a bomb in the World Trade Center garage, planned by the al-Qaeda-trained terrorist Ramzi Yousef. Six people are killed and a thousand-plus wounded, damage far short of Yousef's later-reported hope of collapsing the North Tower into the South Tower and killing tens of thousands in protest of American support for Israel and interference in the rest of the Middle East. Although the next day's *Times* will have a rare front-page full-banner headline about the bombing, whose culprits are not yet known, it doesn't slow down prep and is not even a small part of my thoughts over the coming months. I don't recall anyone else making anything of it, either.

The movie's start date shifts later (*pushes*, as I learn to say) by a week, and then by another week. It is a period movie, so the art and costume departments need extra time to get everything in place. Or maybe it has to do with an actor's availability. Whatever the cause, it's fine by me, as it's a few more weeks of paid work. The location manager, however, decides to leave the job early to return to his TV series, whose new season is suddenly overlapping with the final weeks of our schedule. It is the only series regularly and fully filmed in New York, its jobs are coveted, and he has a wife, kids, and a house in the suburbs. Bypassing a steady gig for a few weeks or even months of work on a feature film isn't an option, he says. But I am given to understand his departure will not be mourned and, though he has suggested a departure date to the production manager, she tells him he will be replaced immediately. I remember hearing him ask her if he will still receive his completion. I don't know what completion is but will learn soon that members of the Directors Guild of America (the DGA) are paid one additional week's salary at the end of a job, called completion of assignment. I don't know if the production manager agrees to pay it, or if it is even up to her. I do know that there is a ruthlessness to the business of film production. I was fired from the first and only other movie I worked on, a low-budget mob movie poorly conceived and never released. A few days later I was hired back due to my replacement's even more extreme incompetence and, I imagine, the difficulty of finding yet another replacement due to the crappy pay, which was less than I'm getting at my lesser position on *Quiz Show*.

The location manager who takes over has great acuity, organizational and personnel skills, and a dry take on the world that I find fully amusing. I appreciate the decision to get her started right away. She reorganizes and expands the department and doles out clear assignments. She comes from the Woody Allen / Martin Scorsese contingent of film workers, a New York nexus that provides the only regular working alternative to the TV series, as Woody (as this group calls that director) shoots a movie in or around New York every year and Scorsese pops up periodically.

During director scouts I notice drivers alongside us doing double takes. Some flashing something has caught their eye. A glimpse of profile? Blond hair? Posture? Amazing how rapid and slight it has been. And then a big smile, a wave, an exclamation. It really is Robert Redford.

———

As day one of shooting nears, I am assigned a location to gaff. This means I am there whenever the prep crew needs to be there. I clean and stock bathrooms, buy snack food and drinks for those getting the location ready, order and pick up lunches, acquire local filming permits, and compile lists of local services in case anyone needs it: dry cleaners, hardware stores, lumberyards, restaurants. With careful guidance from the location manager and her assistant managers (these have multiplied), I will track down support spaces for things like catering and the holding of extras, as well as striking deals and getting contracts signed.

My location is the stand-in for the NBC lobby and executive offices whose occupants hatch the scheme to fix the quiz show and through which almost all the central players of the movie at some time or another pass. The building is in Jersey City. Called Murdoch Hall, it is the location the designer on first seeing photos got most excited about, his initial in-person visit not a disappointment. Its period terrazzo floors, gleamingly detailed deco doorways, banisters, built-ins, and furnishings are of practically priceless value to the production. It had been a nurse's dormitory for the multi-structure medical facility Jersey City's longtime mayor Frank Hague built starting in the late 1920s, about a third of the way through his thirty-year run as one of the most powerful and corrupt politicians in the country. I'll spend a couple months there between prep, shoot, and wrap with carpenters, painters, set dressers, and the pre-lighting, shooting, and wrapping crews. The company will shoot there for a couple weeks during which I will be the point person for anyone on the crew needing access or information.

With the busy exception of the emergency room out the back door of our location, most of the buildings in the complex are empty and held in trust by a nonprofit organization, to whom the production donates money as a location fee and whose building manager, Jim, becomes the person I go to for building access and approval. Jim is short, bullish, and gruff. He personifies the political machine whose old-school ways still permeate Hudson County politics, though I'm rarely confronted with an overt expression of this ethos. There's no doubt about where we are, though, when it's decided that we'll shoot an exterior a few blocks away from Murdoch and will need a street closure, this decision occurring mid-shoot and arrangements needing to be hastily made. I call the police lieutenant I have been dealing with about such permissions, and despite the late notice he tells me he'll make it work, instructing me to have $500 in cash ready and to give a call a couple hours before we want his help. The time comes, and I make the call; not long after I hear my name on the walkie and am told I'm wanted out front. A sergeant, sitting in the passenger seat of a police cruiser, rolls down the window as I approach.

"You have it?" he asks.

"Yes," I say. "Should I get in?"

"Don't bother." He puts his hand out.

I take the cash out of my pocket and turn it over, watching as he counts it. He soon nods and rolls his window back up, the patrol car speeding off. A few of the teamsters sitting outside laugh when I walk back past them.

"Haven't seen that in a while," one of them says.

I was born in the maternity hospital a couple of buildings east of Murdoch Hall. We have set up our catering room on its ground floor. There's a private apartment on the top floor, a grand view of Manhattan out its east-facing windows. Margaret Hague Maternity Hospital was named for the mayor's mother. The apartment was built for his mistress.

The whole complex is a mess of peeling paint, water-stained ceilings, and swampy basements. The elevators are iffy, and during shoot days we'll have a mechanic on standby at a pricey hourly rate. Murdoch Hall itself is full of elaborate and weighty art deco lamps, tables, chairs, desks, and other substantial pieces. The set decorator sets aside what the set dressers will clean up for use in the offices and the lobby, stashing it all in a large room at the back of the building also used as their shop.

One day coming back up the walk from an errand I see two scenic artists — they are romantic partners — carrying out a weighty period side table. I watch as they load it into their personal truck.

"Stuff is going to waste here," one of them tells me as he heads back toward the building.

"Don't let Jim see you," I say.

"Jim's been selling the stuff to the set dressers as fast as they can load it out," the other one says.

A few minutes later, I see them carting out the matching side table.

The leadman is the person in charge of the movie's massive crew of set dressers. He shows up periodically to check his team's progress. The set dressers clean up the dusty rooms, polish the terrazzo floors and wainscoting, hang pictures and curtains, move appropriate furniture into the offices, and then place pens, pencils, paper, coatracks, and photographs around to give the offices a realistic sense of clutter and personality. Joe is the gang boss, the top dresser at the location, in charge of the day-to-day assignments for the eight or ten set dressers there for the early weeks of prep, a number that grows to twenty or more as the first day of filming at Murdoch approaches. Gravel-voiced, dry, droll, big, and strong, Joe alternates teasing and teaching me. He can almost always be found around the building engaged in some chore on one of the sets or in the shop. He likes an audience and always engages with me when I show up.

He might say, "I saw Jim going off on you there, the fucking tool."

Or, talking about the breakfast food I pick up every morning for his team, he'll say, "You know you don't have to bother with the fancy donuts. Just go to Dunkin' for these animals."

I'm particularly amused when these conversations happen across an ironing board, Joe carefully spreading drapery on its surface and gently pressing the hot iron down, or with him behind a sewing machine, cutting and hemming, his large hands moving with precision as he continues to cackle and curse.

His boss is twice as foulmouthed and consistently sarcastic, with no time for Joe's occasional kindness. If I come across him when he's with Joe or another of the dressers, he'll make a crack.

"He thinks he's gonna grow up to be a producer," he says about me on multiple occasions.

"You wanna be a producer, Kamine? Fat fucking chance."

"Whatever you say," is about as much of a fight as I put up.

Joe laughs along with his boss. But I feel he's only about half on board.

At the end of the day I go back to the office in the city to turn around my petty cash envelope, drop off contracts or check requests, and give the location manager an update on the work being done. On day one of principal photography at a location in Manhattan, I drive to the set as I have some contracts that need countersignatures. I follow the TO SET signs to the building's service entrance, where one of the location assistants tells me we've just wrapped. I'm at the freight elevator when the door opens, and Redford, the first assistant director, the director of photography, and a few others instantly march out, forcing me back a few steps. They have a new look in their eyes: charged up, fierce, focused. The casualness that had been a reliable part of Redford's manner during prep is nowhere in sight.

A week or two before filming at Murdoch Hall starts, the riggers come in to hang pipe grids, cables, and lights above the office sets, the lights encased in diffusion-wrapped frames called soft boxes. The set dressing crew continues to grow. Other departments come by, too. Costumes moves in racks and background clothing, and I set up makeup stations in an unused room on the second floor. The location manager has decided there are too many people working there for one person to handle. She sends over another location assistant to help and says she's hiring a two-person craft service team to deal with the food and drinks as prep finishes, asking if I know anyone who'd be interested.

At home that night I call my friend Mike from film school and ask if he'd do it.

"Sure," he says.

"You think Mike might be into it, too?" I say. There were two Mikes in my class.

"Lemme ask," Mike says.

He calls me back with a yes. I give him Murdoch's address, and when they show up the next morning I give them the tour and the Sam's Club card for bulk purchases.

Later that week the location manager comes by to look things over. Seeing the spread Mike and Mike have set up, she stops to talk to them. She likes them. She doesn't like the craft service crew the former location manager has left her with, and she's thinking of making a change.

"Do you guys want to stay on?" she asks them.

"Are you kidding?" Mike says.

"Of course," the other Mike says.

She goes over what the shooting crew will expect from them. They'll finish the Murdoch Hall prep and take over from the other team when the shooting crew gets here, then will move on with them for the rest of the job.

I have picked the least-distressed dorm-room floor in the building and subcontracted painters to clean and whitewash the hallway and a dozen of the rooms. It isn't a set, so the union crew is happy not to get involved in scraping the no-doubt-lead-based paint off the crumbling plaster walls. These will be green rooms — where the actors can relax while the set is being lit — furnished with beds, desks, chairs, and rugs.

A few days before filming begins, one of the assistant managers comes out and takes me shopping at the strip mall on the city's perimeter, picking out vases and blankets and other decorations and comforts. We arrange these in the green rooms. I put in a flower order for the morning of the first day of shooting.

At wrap on the Friday before that, Redford, the producer, the DP, and the first assistant director make the trip out to New Jersey to look at the completed lobby and offices. A group of people meets them. The production designer and set decorator showed up hours in advance and have been sprucing up the offices. The gaffer and key grip, the production manager, the location manager, and the assistant location manager who will be covering the shoot days with me arrive just ahead of Redford and the others. When they're all assembled, they take the tour. I follow them around.

"Is the color a little light?" Redford asks once we're all back downstairs at the entrance, looking up and around at the two-tiered lobby.

"It might be, yes," the designer says.

"Definitely," the producer says.

Redford and the core group leave. The designer, set decorator, and charge scenic hang back, looking at color chips. They make a decision. The scenic crew will need to work all weekend, twelve or fourteen hours on Saturday and Sunday, to repaint the entire lobby for Monday morning. They will need a dozen or more painters. The production manager approves the overage. She also relays a few chores she'd like me to take care of, since I'll be there with the painters anyway. She doesn't look at me as she's talking. In the stairwell that leads to the side exit she points up at the peeling paint and flaking plaster, some of which drifts down over the course of each day. I mop it up every morning.

"You could've mentioned this," she says to me. "It's a problem. I'm sending carpenters in this weekend to box it in. Are there other places people might walk through that look like this?"

"Maybe the back door," I say.

"Look around the whole place before you leave today and look at what's above your head," she says. "Anything that looks like this, show the carpenters when they're here so they can contain it."

Two location production assistants stand outside a cargo van smoking cigarettes when I pull up at 4:00 AM Monday, three hours before the general crew call. The van holds tables and chairs, extension cords, mops, brooms, buckets, butt cans for the smokers in the cast and crew, rolls of paper towels and toilet paper, additional makeup mirrors, clip lights, tall bi-folded wooden frames wrapped in duvetyne that serve as changing areas for extras. Filming will commence after a frantic load-in and the flurry of requests from departments for spaces to keep equipment close by but out of range of the camera. There will be questions about what windows open so cable can be snaked into the building, where bathrooms can be found, how to get the camera truck closer, why the director's trailer is right outside the building and we get stuck pushing our shit up a goddamn hill, why there isn't more parking for crew cars closer to this dump, and who picked New Jersey for the biggest set in the movie anyway?

"Locations," I hear over the walkie when someone has a question or command for my department, in this case meaning me.

"Locations, come see Michael."

"Come see Joe."

"Come see Dennis."

"Locations, go to channel two."

"Locations . . ."

On day two I'm called to the set to see the producer, the man I worked for free for and who put me on the movie. He's sitting in a director's chair outside the office we'll be filming that morning.

"Oh, hey Mark," he says. "Listen, you have a contact at the hospital out back?"

I nod.

"Good," he says. "Good. Hey, would you mind asking them to ask their ambulance drivers to cut their sirens when they pull down the emergency-room alleyway?"

"Turn their sirens off?" I say.

"Yeah. Thanks."

He's already looking away. Redford is coming off the set having checked the first camera setup.

I do not talk to my contact at the hospital. Toward the end of the day the location manager shows up to see how things are going. I tell her what the producer asked me to do and she says, "You didn't do it, did you?"

"No," I say.

"Good. Don't."

By the third day at Murdoch the crew has settled in and the requests for location assistance are slowing. I watch scenes get shot if they're out in the lobby, but the longer scenes take place in the various offices, where only essential people are welcome: director, actors, DP, camera operator and focus puller, boom operator, and a few hands in case a light or flag (a black cloth on a rectangular metal frame used to cut light off walls or actors or the camera) needs to be moved.

There's a video feed to a monitor placed off set, out in a hallway, and people stand around it behind the lineup of directors' chairs, watching takes with the producers and occasional guests seated beside them. Usually hair and makeup are there. Redford sometimes stays on set with the actors and camera operators, sometimes watches from his chair in front of the monitor. While extended lighting changes occur, he goes out front to his trailer or takes the elevator up to his green room, which he uses more and more as the company's tenure at Murdoch Hall extends and word gets out to fans and reporters, who wait on the sidewalk for a glimpse of him, hoping for photos or autographs or a word or a smile.

I see the actors get out of cars or vans and head into the building, escorted by the first-team PA (*first team* meaning "cast," and *PA* meaning "production assistant"). The hair and makeup people arrive alongside them or en masse in a following van, sitting off set on their low-slung, easy-carry folding chairs until called in for "last looks," addressing their charges' raised faces with brushes and wands and lipsticks. If they have time to kill, the cast will talk together, say hello to crew they're getting to know, look to catch Redford's eye, stand alongside the producer at the monitor. A couple of them, maybe more method in their approach or not having fully learned their lines, stand alone, murmuring.

I also see them in the green-room hallway upstairs where they, too, are learning to hide between scenes, and sometimes in the catering room down the block. One day the young star of the movie, Ralph Fiennes, unknown at the time but with a key role in Spielberg's Holocaust movie to be released later that year, sits down across from me. I see that he's reading *All the Pretty Horses*, the Cormac McCarthy novel that has made the author suddenly widely known. He was a favorite of many of the writers in the fiction-writing workshops I participated in during the 1980s. My friend J. D. Dolan is a big fan. I have not read *Horses* but have read around in some earlier ones, *Suttree* especially, without much interest, an opinion I do not express to my writing friends. When Fiennes looks up, I ask what he thinks of the novel, implying familiarity.

"It's astonishingly visual," he says. "He makes you see everything."

"He's an intense writer," I say.

Murdoch becomes a kind of location department social club, the manager and the couple of other assistant managers making the trip out to New Jersey toward the end of each shoot day. I listen to the manager talk on her cell phone to assistants at upcoming locations, to the accountant or production manager or producers, to the scouts still working. I admire again her strategies for calmly, drolly dealing with what comes along. I particularly enjoy her interchanges over the walkie with the second assistant director, who is equally seasoned and equally droll but more insistent, impatient, and prying. A tall, stooped, lugubrious-looking man with the same first name as the first AD, Joe – causing everyone to run his first and single-syllable

last name together whenever referring to him – is full of tales
of his eccentric childhood as one of a dozen or so children of the
mayor of Buffalo, New York, whose mother got his birthdate
wrong for years and whose father each Christmas lined up the
children and after asking for their names and ages passed out
the year's cash gift. This Joe calls the location manager's name
out on the walkie frequently when he learns she's on site.

"Amy locations, what's your twenty?" he will say over the
walkie.

"Joe B, go to two," she will reply. She flips her walkie to
channel two and, after he confirms he's there, says, "What do
you want, Joe B?"

"What's your twenty, Amy?"

"What do you want?" she says again.

"I want to know where you are."

"That's on a need-to-know basis," she says.

This back-and-forth can go on for a while. She won't tell
him where she is, knowing he really does not need to know.
Sometimes we are near the set, in the small superintendent's
office tucked behind the elevator bank that we're using as our
location work space. More and more often, as the company's
stay at Murdoch extends and the big issues are ironed out and
things are running smoothly, we are on the roof, twenty-two
floors up, with a grill borrowed from the Mikes, folding chairs
from the location van, Amy or one of the assistant managers
organizing shopping trips for burgers, hot dogs, steaks, and
the great local sausage breads from an Italian bakery up the
hill. Bottles of wine and even pitchers of sangria are wrangled
for the first Friday night. The following week, the last we'll
shoot at Murdoch, the wine and sangria come out earlier in
the week and we elaborate on the menu, with fresh seafood
marinating before grilling, vegetables cut up and oiled and
grilled as side dishes. Most of the department shows up, half

a dozen making the trip out at the end of prep days in the city. There is a great team feeling to it. This is another quality of the manager – encouraging this bond – that I admire and make note of.

The local film commissioner tells me Jim Florio, New Jersey's governor, wants to stop by to meet Redford. I tell the producer who hired me, and he okays it once Redford consents. I am the contact person because no one wants to deal with it.

The day comes. State police show up to look around ahead of Florio's arrival. Next come the film commissioner, the county executive, a small band of advisers. One of them decides, since the governor is pulling up out front and Redford is nowhere in sight, that a tour of the sets might be a good idea. Florio, trim, handsome, hurried, is introduced, and after I explain that Bob (this is how we all refer to Redford) will be down in a bit, I begin the set tour. Florio partakes with polite lack of interest.

Fifteen minutes later we are standing around in the lobby. Crew members sweep by in twos and threes, carrying gear, talking into walkies, not interested enough to give the group more than a quick look. There's nothing to do, and Redford hasn't shown up. I know based on chatter over the walkie he's up on the green-room floor, but his assistant isn't answering me, and as the silence and Florio's inexpressiveness are prolonged, I decide to go upstairs. The assistant meets me at the elevator. She tells me she told Bob that Florio is downstairs and then waves me to the threshold of Redford's green room, where I find him lying on the narrow bed against the far wall, his head propped up on an elbow, smoking a cigarette.

"Seems I have to do this," he says.

"I could make an excuse," I say.

He shakes his head, stands up.

The governor is waiting at the elevator bank, and he and

Redford instantly break away from the others and walk across the lobby, talking. Redford leads Florio into an office and closes the door. They spend ten or fifteen minutes there, enough time that the set that shoots next is now lit and the actors are waiting, the first AD having sent a PA over to stand outside the closed door. Eventually it opens, and Redford leads Florio out. They shake hands. Redford follows the PA to set. The governor and those who came in with him head to the exit. His people seem satisfied. They say thanks before leaving.

Filming at Murdoch finishes, and a few weeks later the wrap is winding down. The painters have filled in and touched up scrapes and scratches, and everything except the sold-off or stolen furniture is back in place. The set dressers polished and buffed the floors. I do a final walk-through with Jim, the building manager, and Joe, the lead set dresser. Jim points out things he feels need more work. He wants his people to do the rest. He'll get me bids and we'll make checks out directly to the vendors, but regardless I'm guessing that Jim will finally be able to get kickbacks, something the movie crew's self-sufficiency, beyond the painting and scraping of the green-room floor, has deprived him of. As we near the end of the walk-through, Jim offers to take me out on his boat, berthed at the marina in downtown Jersey City. "Half hour and you're out in the wide-open seas off Point Pleasant," he says. "Nothing like it."

I see Joe smiling at the idea of me spending leisure time with the guy.

"Sounds great, Jim," I say.

He has reestablished himself in the grandest of the offices on the mezzanine, his base before we took over. At the end of my last day at Murdoch I hand over my set of keys and an envelope

I've prepared. Jim opens it and stares at what is inside, his look of confusion soon turning dark. It's a $350 gift certificate from Bloomingdale's.

"What's this for?" he says.

"It's for you, Jim, from the movie. Or for your wife."

After a long silence, noticeably not a happy one, he launches into a loud excoriation of my lack of appreciation for all the work he put into accommodating us. It is an insult. I am an ingrate, a punk, and we are a low-class operation.

I tell Jim it's all they let us do for people, or something along these lines. "It's not us, it's Disney. I know it's not the way to do things, but we don't have a choice."

He pushes the envelope back across his desk at me.

"Don't you think your wife would like it?" I say.

"You people disgust me," he says. "If I'd have known this was what would come of it, I would've told the county to send you packing. Get out of my sight before I get up and come around this desk."

I decide I will mail it to him later, for him to keep or tear up, and I do, and don't hear another word. When I come across Joe later that day, he gets a big kick out of telling me he and his guys heard Jim yelling at me from down in the lobby. Then Joe paints the picture of the post-gift-certificate boat ride Jim will take me on, weights and chains ready belowdecks.

The job rolls on. I cover a few more locations. They are all less intensive and complicated than Murdoch. The company will prep each for a few days and shoot for a day or two. I spend a week of prep in an apartment on 106th Street in Manhattan that will be the home of the young lawyer investigating the scandal and his wife, played by Rob Morrow and Mira Sorvino, where I admire the no-nonsense and athletic efficiency with which a rigging grip team comes in to black out the upper-floor windows (most of the apartment scenes take place at night but will be shot during the day). At some point during one of the first shoot days there I find myself tucked against a wall to stay out of camera range and in response to a frantic call to shut off the noisy temporary air-conditioning whose compressor is an arm's length away, I reach out and hit the toggle switch. The moment cut is called, one of the crew, hovering over me, tells me that I have violated union rules by touching the AC and to keep the fuck away from the equipment or he'll have me thrown off set.

The prep and shoot days are long for locations, but I have a decent amount of downtime when I'm not with the shooting crew and always have a book with me, happy to tell whoever bothers to ask what I'm reading, after I tip up the book to show them, and that I write book reviews for a magazine called *The New Leader*, though it's hardly a magazine, just thirty or so semi-gloss sheets of paper stapled together and enclosing some name reviewers loyal to its mildly glorious past. No one shows much interest. But having caught wind of my writing sideline, the location manager asks me to write a letter to someone at the state department in the hope of getting permission to film some scenes at a federal building in Washington, DC. The permission is granted, and I accept the manager's and even the producer's praise for my work, though I suspect mentioning Robert Redford in the first sentence was the only rhetorical skill required.

Near the end of the job the first location manager, who'd left the job early, reaches out to offer me work as a scout on the TV show. I'll make over a thousand dollars a week, a big raise.

I seem to have found a way into the film business.

3

Crime Series

Not long after *Quiz Show*, I've moved up and am working as an assistant location manager on a network TV crime series. We gather in the office to regroup after an episode's on-location work is done. It's as relaxed as it gets in the ongoing churn of TV production, a season of twenty-two or twenty-three episodes, each episode shooting for seven or eight days while the one to follow is being prepped. The location department has a manager (Bart, one of the best of the *Quiz Show* scouts) and two assistant managers (a New York locations regular and me). The company finishes the shooting of each episode with three or four days of stage work. The prep for the episode to follow is being covered by Bart and the other assistant location manager. This is the time when the two on-set assistants and I can catch our breath, sifting through our backpacks for location contracts collected during shooting and filling out petty cash envelopes into which we insert gas and second-meal and parking receipts. We also always have a few cash disbursement forms to turn in. Known as bribe forms, they are filled out to account for cash handed out to coax construction workers to stop work while we roll sound, to calm angry store owners because our trucks have eaten up all the nearby parking, to get a superintendent to let our actors exit from a doorway that the director has decided is better than simply finding them walking down the sidewalk. The bribe forms have slots for dollar amount, reason for payment, name, address, Social Security number, and signature. We are expected to give out as little as we can get away with, $20 or $50 or worst case $100. Beyond that amount we need to get Bart or a producer to sign off.

There are people here or there who don't want to give out their personal information.

"I'm not signing nothing," a super might say. "Gimme the fifty bucks or the cable's not going in my alleyway."

Or, "I'll turn my music off but you're not getting my Social," from the second-floor tenant with a speaker pointed out his window, wise to what a film shoot will pay for silence.

A location assistant might tell me he can't get the super/merchant/asshole to sign.

"Wait here a sec," I say. I walk over to tell the producer at the monitor. The first AD and the director are usually there, too.

"They won't give us a Social Security number," I say.

"Give it to him anyway," the producer says.

I go back over. "Do it," I tell the assistant.

We always get the okay — anything to not slow down the shooting day. Soon we don't ask. We hand over the cash and write down the business name or building address and, back at the office, get the fold-creased form out of our backpack and invent a name or Social Security number to go with the reason for payment. Bart understands, the producer knows it happens, the accountants have nothing to say.

We have reverse telephone directories to look up an address and get the name and number of a resident or owner, useful for scouts when the designer or director points out a building of interest as we drive around the city. We realize it's equally easy to use the directory to find an address near where we shot and get a real name, address, and phone number to put on a bribe form. From there it's a short step to creating bribe forms for money never handed out. You make up a Social Security number and decide on the amount and reason for payment. I don't remember how far I push it, but two or three invented bribes per episode become commonplace in my petty cash envelopes, and the location assistants and the other assistant manager are clocking about the same. We scratch out a few practice signatures on a notepad, changing the way we make F's or L's or S's and the slant of our script, and then autograph the bogus forms for one another. It adds $100 or $150 to our earnings every couple weeks and, even better, it's cash.

I recall the production manager on a small movie I'd done before the crime series saying, after initialing one of my at-that-time fully legitimate envelopes, "Petty cash – you can't get rich on it, but you can make a decent living."

My wife and I have been spending weekends looking for a house. Jack is three years old. The apartment with the office up front feels small. His two-hour-a-day, three-day-a-week nursery school is sweet, lovely, and cooperative – and costs thousands of dollars per semester. We've begun the stress-filled sorting of public elementary school options, knowing if that doesn't work out we'll need to put him in private school. My wife's business is solid and I'm doing better, but private school will be a stretch, and we don't seem to be digging in quite as deeply as our friends in pursuing the public option. And we want more space. A lawn, a neighborhood, a community. We want what we grew up with, it seems. What we spend half our weekly therapy sessions recovering from.

Westchester is too expensive. Long Island is unimaginably congested and for Tana full of landmine memories. New Jersey, which Tana once joked she wanted ruled out by a prenup, loses some of its stigma when we bump into a fellow graphic designer, her husband a well-known illustrator, who tells us they've just bought a house in Montclair.

We look across the river and find the perfect house. We are outbid. We look at thirty more and take an interest in one with dense overgrown hedges obfuscating its façade and wall-to-wall pea-green carpeting covering its half a dozen rooms. It's on a cute street with a tree-strewn center island. The fixes are cosmetic, we figure. We make an offer and to our surprise get it. We will move into it in December if we can get a mortgage. Our accountant, a government-hating hippie living on the top floor of a public housing complex on the Upper West Side, stacks of homemade cassette tapes covering every surface, tells us he'll lie on the bank forms, adding that the last time he did this the overextended couple missed payments and lost the house to foreclosure.

"Thanks for the encouragement, Fred," my wife says.

I keep the petty cash scam rolling.

The TV show's production designer has a cynical attitude toward the second-tier cop show we're making, if not toward the whole business. His pride or design sense or need to keep the paychecks coming in thwarts him from simply signing off on poor or lazy or nonsensical decisions. He is particularly cutting and dismissive of our two producers, whose high-handed stewardship is entirely unchecked by the showrunner and writers in LA.

One day the designer walks me over to the newly opened Chelsea Market, an early retail conversion of a massive industrial building, now home to appealing butcher, seafood, and baked goods shops among dozens of empty spaces beckoning tenants. We shoot there sometimes, in loft-like empty upper floors or after hours in the brick-and-steel corridors of the market itself, good for scenes of surreptitious meetings or the discovery of bodies and drug labs.

"Check this out," the designer says.

We have stopped in front of a unit close to the Ninth Avenue entrance of the market where a couple of our carpenters are at work.

"Is this for something in the new beat sheet?" I say, referring to the outlines we get so we can prep when a script is late.

"It's not for the show," he says. "It's going to be a real liquor store."

I take a closer look. I see pricey lumber stacked on the floor, some counters and wine racks already up, our guys cutting and measuring.

"Holy shit," I say. "It's . . ."

I name our two producers.

"Exactly," the designer says. "I drew up the plans. We're building it and charging it to sets, spreading the cost out over the episodes."

"Pretty bold," I say.

"It's a fucking disgrace," the designer says. "But it will be a beautiful store."

The producers don't normally scout locations with us, unless their boss back in LA has granted one of them an episode to direct, but we often get calls in the van from their assistant asking what neighborhood we'll be in at lunchtime. We tell her and she hangs up, calling back a few minutes later.

The assistant might tell us to meet at Nobu at 1:00 PM.

Or Union Square Café.

Or some other high-end, pricey place.

We eat ridiculously well. The enormous bills for eight or nine people that go on my credit card garner me tons of bonus points. Sometimes after these meals, the senior producer wants someone to join him in his car to continue a conversation or to go look at something on the way back to the office and asks for company, and now and then that means me. He's a fast and somewhat distracted driver, enjoys talking about high-end audio or video gear, new gadgets, stock market picks, and anything we pass that catches his eye. I sit in the passenger seat trying not to straighten my leg too abruptly to brace myself for a crash that never happens.

In early December, halfway through the show's first season, we move into our house in Montclair. It's Saturday, December 10, 1994. That day, as we read a few days later in *The New York Times*, a man is killed by an explosive device in North Caldwell, a couple of towns over. Eventually Unabomber Ted Kaczynski will claim responsibility and justify this act as retaliation for public relations work the man's firm did to smooth over the bad press surrounding the *Exxon Valdez* oil spill.

A few months after that, on a Tuesday afternoon, there's a shooting at the Watchung Plaza post office, which is a short walk from our house. That night we don't sleep well. The next day we learn that four people were killed and they don't know who did it. Thoughts of a lunatic with a gun roaming the neighborhood are with us for the next few days. When they catch the suspect, an ex-postal-employee with a grudge, we relax. But we wonder about this move to the suburbs. I'll learn later that Tana has had a couple months of crying jags. Before the move she'd lived in the city for nearly twenty years, since transferring to Pratt Institute halfway through college, so I understand the feeling of dislocation without knowing what to do about it. A few times she's crying when I leave in the morning and crying when I get home at night. My eyes must widen because she says, "I wasn't like this all day."

The crime series runs for four seasons. I work on three of them. I am one of two assistant location managers for seasons one and two, then become the manager when Bart gets bumped up to production manager. As assistant manager I make $1,800 a week, and when I become the manager, I make about $1,000 more. I work twelve or so hours a day when prepping an episode. Sixteen hours isn't unusual on location days. The twenty-two- or twenty-three-episode season means forty or so weeks of employment each year. In between seasons I might have some time off but take jobs on movies or pilots when offered. We're still carrying credit card debt and my student loans.

During the series I am in frequent contact with the designer and set decorator, so even before the liquor store subterfuge starts, I am aware of other scams far more substantial than my petty cash petty larceny. The Mission furniture bought for a location that ends up furnishing one producer's uptown pied-à-terre (he lives in Westchester). The sleek digital German stereo system and its high-powered speakers purchased for a swing set that shoots for one day then gets delivered to the other producer's West Village town house. And there's the day I am summoned into the senior producer's office and asked if I've noticed what's going on on the West Side Highway.

"The construction?" I say. I wonder if it's a concern about traffic patterns or noise we might hear during filming on the stage.

"Yeah, yeah, the construction," the producer says. "Notice anything about it?"

After a moment's thought I say, "Never knew there were pavers under there."

Also known as Belgian block, pavers are still the surface material on some of the streets near the office. I remember wondering if they were everywhere beneath the black-tar-bound macadam of New York when I saw them revealed beneath the highway.

"They're throwing it out," the producer says. "I stopped and asked. Can you fucking believe it?"

"Crazy," I say. I really have no problem believing it.

"Maybe send someone down there in the cargo van with a few hundred bucks," he says as he writes something down. "See what they'll take for a load? Have them deliver it to this place."

It's the Fort Lee, New Jersey, address of a friend of his who is redoing his driveway and patio. The workers happily take $300 in cash, and the next time the producer has us rent a pickup truck for better haulage. I forget how many loads it takes to satisfy the friend's demand.

At some point during the final season of the series, the producers' illicit behavior catches up with them, the studio auditors having uncovered the liquor store scam or something similar. I'm no longer there, but an assistant location manager calls me the day security shows up, relieving both men of their keys and escorting them off the premises, ignoring their protests and not letting them pick up their computers and other personal possessions. Soon after, the locks are changed and a couple of people are brought in to cover the final episodes and shut the production down. The series will not be renewed.

The senior of the two was occasionally amusing and chummy and even funny, and the other could take you into his confidence with a kind of gruff grace, and so the chatter about their overdue exodus isn't entirely fueled by glee, but no one I speak to about it seems upset. Both men spend years banished in practice if not in fact from the business, then make brief and not particularly notable reappearances years later.

– 4 –

My *Sopranos* Years, Part One

I meet David Chase on the streetside dining area of a midtown hotel. It's 1998 and he's fifty-two. Although he has won two Emmys by now and has a long list of credits, mostly for writing, he's not what anyone would call famous. He wears, probably, a button-down shirt open at the neck, a sports jacket, dark slacks, dark shoes. He is clean-shaven, with short hair getting sparse at the top and shot through with gray, or so I remember it. He has a high forehead, slightly aquiline nose, slightly sunken cheeks. He doesn't say much. When he does, he speaks rapidly and without affect. He also listens to what you say and, you get the sense, evaluates. I am there to be evaluated, as the pilot he shot the prior year has after months of waiting been picked up and it's time to get the early crew hires done for season one.

Word is the pilot was not easy. They had some very long shoot days, a standard that episodic TV pilots are known for, given they have more at stake, are typically helmed by highly in-demand and demanding directors, and have big budgets and ambitious originative scripts. David was the pilot's director as well as writer. I was told that well into the shoot on one of those long days, under pressure from a producer or assistant director or simply feeling what was in the air, in a rare moment of visible temper, he had broken away from shot setup and actor coaching and other director-related tasks to give a speech insisting that they would take the time to get things right, budgets and producer and studio mandates be damned, a goal in retrospect clearly achieved.

I know they had rough going with locations. During the prep of the pilot, while I was on another job, I got calls from my old film school classmate Mike K. He was brought on by Bill Barvin, a *Quiz Show* scout who did the pilot's early scouting and escorted David to locations, and someone – David, or the line producer, or the production manager – had decided to give Bill a shot at managing. He was a great scout, maybe the best in the city. He was tall and gawky, with longish side-parted greasy black hair, a large nose, a pockmarked face. He spoke with deliberation and confidence, and had been at it for years, so I can understand construing him as a management candidate. He was certainly a great person to have on your team when needing to know quickly what was out there and when looking for hard-to-find stuff. He was never going to succeed as a location manager, though. Deliberateness in speech and manner are useless. You need to make quick decisions and deals. You need to intuit when a property owner's hesitation or slow response is a sign that things will not work out and then quickly plant the seed with the production designer or director, who will get annoyed if something that has been checked off the endless list of pre-production duties is suddenly back on it. You need to be able to run the half a dozen or more people in your department and delegate tasks. And then on tech scouts and in the other final prep phases before shooting begins, you need to set parameters for the crew, not one of whom cares about the anxiety and disruption visited upon location owners on a shoot day or about the impact the invasion of a hundred or more people and the dozen or so trucks that go along with them has not only on the store or apartment or office or auto body shop that is to be filmed but also on the neighboring businesses and residences. Scouting is a honeymoon period, and the skills of a scout — enthusiasm, salesmanship, an artistic eye — are in almost all ways antithetical to the blunt assessments and cost-cutting strategies essential to the business of location managing. At a certain point Bill was shunted aside and an experienced location manager on the cusp of moving up but needing a job was called in to take over, under the slightly elevated if ambiguous title of unit manager, a real job in some countries but without specific meaning in the United States. I will be in touch with him as I prep to learn what there is to learn about the places shot on the pilot that will recur in the series' first season.

My meeting with David doesn't last long. I don't remember details of the conversation. Ilene, the pilot's line producer and now a producer on the series, is at his side, to gauge how I'm doing and for post-meeting feedback, I imagine. She had called me for the pilot but I was on another job. I'd worked with her a couple of times before. She will, for the seven seasons of *The Sopranos* that will ultimately be filmed (the seventh, for some contractual or creative reason, called season six part two), remain sedulously at David's side, mostly in support of his aims and occasionally, and more and more rarely with the show's growing success, as a check to extravagance. Her position will evolve from the standard line-producing tasks of wrangling the budget, hiring and overseeing the crew, and mediating between creative needs and studio constraints to something more elevated and nebulous as success and ambition thicken upper-echelon staffing. She will have increased creative input and become a central voice in marketing and merchandising, areas line producers usually only touch on tangentially.

I read the pilot script. For a while some months back, I had been talking to a producer about location managing Harold Ramis's feature film starring Robert De Niro and Billy Crystal,

Analyze This, so what initially strikes me about *The Sopranos* is the unlikelihood of coming across another project with a mob boss whose anxiety causes him to seek out a shrink.

I also watch the working cut of the pilot. Ilene has relayed that according to the studio it has tested well with "women and professors." I can't say I get it at first. I admire certain aspects of it right away: the transplanting of the Scorsese-like brutality of urban mobsters into green and spacious suburban settings, as in the daylight office park assault on an indebted medical executive; the restraint and subtlety of the interwoven plotlines; the great naturalism of James Gandolfini and Edie Falco, noticeably more natural and persuasive than many of the sidekicks, whose performances feature physical mugging and emotive exaggerations that for me at least take some getting used to. Not that anyone cares what I think. And not that it really matters to me, either. It is a long, well-paying job. I am happy to have it.

No one is used to HBO or the other cable TV channels making their own shows. It is a place you turn to for sporting events and movies after their theatrical runs. When doing the initial scouting and looking to induce interest in location owners, we get nowhere by explaining we'll be filming a New Jersey mob drama for a cable TV channel. Invoking James Gandolfini draws blanks. Michael Imperioli, who plays Christopher Moltisanti, was the kid shot in the foot in *Goodfellas*, for what that's worth. Lorraine Bracco, who portrays Dr. Jennifer Melfi, is the best we have to offer. People know who she is or are familiar enough with the name to put the face in place when you simply add: The wife in *Goodfellas*. But it isn't exactly like dropping Robert Redford's name.

I have been since moving to Montclair and will remain thanks to my *Sopranos* years a mostly solitary commuter. I ride countless times, in a series of mid-priced cars, all permutations of the fifteen or so crow-flown miles between our house and Silvercup Studios in Long Island City, not infrequently going from New Jersey to Queens and back twice in the same day, clocking up to an hour and a half per leg. I also periodically experience that most miserable of commuting nightmares, the off-hour traffic jam at tunnel or bridge. There is nothing worse than cruising across midtown at midnight only to turn down the 30th Street entrance to the Lincoln Tunnel and find yourself in a lineup of late-night travelers, instantly causing you to wonder what the fuck you did to deserve this. I refuse to add up in even loosely estimated fashion the days of my life I inch along at the entrances to the tunnels and bridges between New York and New Jersey, along with the hours and hours of slow crawls on Routes 3 and 46, the West Side Highway, the Major Deegan Expressway, and the Harlem River Drive. I try with some success to remain calm when traffic slows. There is nothing to be done. I can't take trains or buses as I need my car to make the swoops among all the places I might be required to be during a working day: the set that is being shot, the director scouts for the next episode, an upcoming location or its owner's office or residence if a deal needs to be done in person, the strip club whose owner expects each negotiation to take place face-to-face, the Soprano house location whose owner requires constant coaxing, the occasional city council or mayor's office or planning board meeting when a production representative's presence is mandated to get a variance for late-night shooting or to explain why the cars we're crashing won't hurt anyone. I remember almost nothing of my time in traffic beyond a feeling of frequent barely suppressed anger liable to spew forth in fruitless profanity when I am cut off or, due to unlucky lane selection, passed too frequently or left to wait while the moron in front of me completes a text, which

for much of the period of the late 1990s and early 2000s means
the need to spell out words by pressing a numerical key one,
two, or three times per letter.

I remember not much else, except my stiff discomfort
during the dozens of commutes I make with a Montclair-based
producer. This man is as extremely knowledgeable about
film production as he is unsuited to his role near its pinna-
cle, a not uncommon situation in a field full of the too-ready
acceptance of tantrums, predation, bullying, and nastiness.
Over the course of my career the top production jobs remain
mostly in the hands of men, a solid percentage of them arrogant, boastful, subtly or openly abusive of underlings, and
prone to raising their voices for no good reason. It is many
years before the reckoning will come. That this producer
came up as a first assistant director, a position where blaming
and shaming were once common, fits. First ADs are conduits
for directors' decrees and wishes and organizers of the flow
of cast and crew to and from the set. They are responsible
for the relentless progression of the shooting day. They turn
each script into a shooting schedule before filming starts then
supervise the information that goes into each day's call sheet,
a two-sided piece of legal paper handed out to the crew at wrap
detailing the next day's work. Completing the day's work is
one of the principal things ADs push for. It means getting
actors to set in camera-ready hair, makeup, and wardrobe;
checking that props are standing by, that the lighting setup
is complete, and the camera is in position so "Rolling" can be
called the moment the last star gets to set and the director is
ready to go. Timing is inevitably not perfect, and waiting is
common on film sets. Too much lag time will always cause
impatience in producers and production managers, who will
ask the AD for ongoing estimates on when the camera will
roll. Many don't need nudging to turn the day into a nonstop

narration of what is causing delays, whether it's an actor still sitting in the hair and makeup trailer, a lighting setup taking longer than predicted by the DP, a missing or malfunctioning prop not yet at camera or not working as expected. There's not always a reason to pick out a person to call out or yell at, but sometimes real mistakes are made, and then it is a question of what to let slide, what to deal with gently, and what to make a public scene over. The producer I drive to work is in the camp of those always willing to go public with problems and is furthermore one of those people who preys on weakness. If he perceives any, he makes things unbearable for that person and steadily unpleasant for those nearby. He will, a few seasons into *The Sopranos*, do so in a way or with a frequency and in a tone of voice that Edie Falco finally refuses to let slide and so she tells David she will no longer work with this man present. Word gets out that David has told Ilene to fire him. There is plenty of backroom discussion as this drama plays out, and a feeling of coming relief. We are let down. An armistice is arranged. The producer is banished from Edie's presence for a while. There is talk of an anger management mandate. If it occurs, it does not take.

More damning than his bullying and tantrums is his behavior around the young women who work with him. In the location office we see his constant attentions to our coordinator, an unostentatiously bright and attractive woman with more interest, it turns out, in a music career than movies or TV. I remember distinctly occasions of creepy shoulder-massaging and hair-stroking and the horrified looks my assistants and I exchange as we discuss with the producer whatever excuse he has found for entering our office and standing behind this woman. We ask her if she wants us to tell his boss, or someone at HBO. She doesn't. We learn later someone in the art department has been pestering her, too, insistently asking her on dates, even offering to separate from his wife if she'll say yes to him.

A couple months before the season ends, she tells me she is quitting. I ask her if it has anything to do with the producer. She doesn't respond at first. I tell her we can call human resources, that she will have a legal case and, who knows, maybe end up with enough money to buy herself a kind of musical fellowship for a few years. *That man* does make things unbearable for her, she agrees. The one in the art department hasn't helped. But she isn't interested in getting into a legal battle. She isn't, she confesses, all that interested in the film business.

But that is months away. When I show up at Silvercup Studios to start work the writers are already down the hall outlining season one. My first chores, after I've spoken at length to my predecessor from the pilot, involve checking in with locations likely to come into play in the episodes ahead. I meet with the Sopranos house owner, who complains about leaks in his roof caused by the security lights the crew mounted up there, creating months of detective work and expensive repairs. As a result, he tells me, he has no interest in hosting our or any other film crew ever again. He is a builder by profession. His house is a prime showpiece of his work. I explain that we'll be replicating his home's interior at our stage in the city and will only need access to shoot exteriors, at most maybe needing to put a light inside for a night scene or to have Soprano family members enter and exit the front and back doors, and that if he wants we will steer clear of the roof. In response he notes that the crew also made a mess of his lawn. He is a fanatic about his lawn. I hear him out, chat him up, ask him to think about it, visit again, talk numbers, and get his consent for at least another shoot day or two to see how it goes. Thus the pattern is set for a back-and-forth between us that will last as long as the series, with his price and our interior incursions escalating as the seasons roll on.

The show's strip club – an actual strip club called Satin Dolls in Lodi, New Jersey – is another repeat location with issues. Its owner, Tony, agrees to meet me there midday, asking after we introduce ourselves if I want anything to eat or drink and, when I say no, getting quickly down to business. He is all business, always. Owning strip clubs is not a pleasant pastime, but for someone who knows what they're doing, it gives evidence of paying well. I will get brief, steady looks at it over the years. I will see Tony push people and rules and regulations as far as he can to take away as much cash as can be made. I will see him come to realize that having a vibrant TV show wanting to film at your place a dozen times a year can be good for revenue and not bad for marketing, either. At our first meeting he tells me that we are welcome to film at the club when it is closed. As they are open from 11:00 AM to 2:00 AM seven days a week, I tell him I don't think that will always work. He says he might consider allowing us to buy him out of a lunch now and then if it's early in the week. By early he means Monday or Tuesday. Wednesday lunch he will need more money than he figures we'll be willing to pay. Forget about Thursday and don't even mention Friday. By the end of our run, actor and episode schedules and our ballooning budget will warp and stretch this arrangement, but for starters, anyway, we pretty much stick to it.

He is a bulky bulldog of a man. His short hair changes colors frequently, veering from an unearthly red to something in the brown family and back again. He has done time for tax evasion and maybe something else. His father was associated with the Genovese crime family and so, I learn later, is he. Growing up in Wayne, New Jersey, I heard mob stories and knew kids whose fathers were supposed to be somehow involved, to what extent never clear, though such associations were always carried proudly. My father knew a few real gangsters by face and name from his life in Paterson and the legal business, telling me that he'd once been addressed by Tony Boy Boiardo at the Knoll Country Club in Parsippany. He was making his way through the dining room and spotted Boiardo, who had seen him looking and therefore took the opportunity to say as he walked by, "Good day, counselor."

My father stopped. "How'd you know I was a lawyer?"

"I make it my business to know who people are," Tony Boy said back.

Satin Dolls' Tony has owned strip clubs for a long time in a lot of New Jersey towns, the one in Lodi and another larger one in Secaucus in operation throughout the series' run. He has many schemes over the years, one to open an all-naked club in the strip mall he owns a short distance up the highway. He runs into local resistance and has trouble with licensing, finally gets it going, closes it down, restarts it, eventually shutters it for good. While it's open, I have an invitation to visit but can't bring myself to do it. Uncomfortable enough when we meet at the mostly empty club midafternoon to see the topless women lazily twirling around the poles on stage, me sometimes with the burger and fries he treats me to, not quite able to keep my eyes off the women. I remember taking calls from Tana there. When she asks where she's catching me and I confess I'm at the bar at the strip club, stressing the point that I'm there to make a deal for the next episode, she just laughs. She gets enough of a kick out of it to bring it up more than once when people ask what working on the show is like.

In later years our meetings take place in his office, a converted garage in an apartment building a few miles from the club, where he keeps liquor and supplies and a couple of desks and phones for him and his general manager. Young guys in vans come and go with deliveries. We do our deals, and sometimes I linger to hear about whatever's on his mind. It's almost always money. How much he could get from me if we tried to shut him down on a Thursday night, something we will have to do in season six, Tony making the most of it. How much he could make off *Sopranos* swag if he printed up T-shirts and coffee mugs. He goes through with this when I get word from an HBO lawyer that they won't do anything about it if he doesn't use the show's logo. In no time there's a vitrine near the club's front entrance, the T-shirts, coffee mugs, and other gear unsurprisingly featuring the iconic pistol-shaped r. HBO doesn't pursue it, as Tony probably figured would be the case.

When I talk to him about the plotline featuring an after-hours gambling club, he confesses he once ran one in Jersey City that cleaned up. At our next meeting he says he's thinking about getting back into it. I never feel fully at ease in his office, wondering if it's bugged, and so when Tony floats the idea of getting back into the after-hours racket, I enunciate clearly that it seems risky to me as it's illegal, and anyway why would he do it, doesn't he have all the money he wants?

"Everyone always wants more money, Mark," he tells me.

He lives in a mansion (he's shown me pictures) in Saddle River, New Jersey, a solidly snazzy town where Richard Nixon spent a decade toward the end of his life, where my half sister and her husband worked for a while at a top private school, where filming is not allowed as it creates an eyesore and brings with it unwanted truck traffic and unwelcome strangers. Tony likes to hire limos to drive him and friends down to Atlantic City, where he gambles. He points out his favorite stripper of the moment and his former favorites, but he warns me to steer clear as they're mostly druggie and all other kinds of trouble. He tells me about a nephew he took on as manager until the kid caught a cocaine habit from the hoor he hooked up with. He refers to the women who dance at his clubs as hoors. They pay him to dance, a standard strip-club practice, each woman handing over fifty bucks or so for her four-hour shift. They keep their tips and a share of any bottles they get their lap-dance clients to buy, Cristal champagne at $300 a pop the big-ticket item Tony has them push.

Of other locations filmed for the pilot, the pork store will not work, period. A busy market with its own set of bad memories from film crew invasion, it has the added disincentive of an Elizabeth, New Jersey, address, a little too far from the city for a once-per-episode visit. I don't do much scouting anymore, but for a while, as we wait for scripts, some of the searching falls to me. Driving along the main drag in Kearny, New Jersey, I spot an empty storefront near the central shopping district whose situation at the bottom of an inverted T provides good exterior angles and enough of a downtown feel to make sense as a retail venue. David likes it. I make a deal with the property owner, who recently bought the building with the idea of installing his growing office-cleaning company in it. He already has permits and shows me the metal studs inside that are the first steps toward conversion. I tell him to stop construction and we'll pay his rent somewhere else along with a decent fee for the building. David changes the store's name from Centanni's to Satriale's. The production designer places matching café tables out front and a bracket-suspended pig up above. The change of venue from pilot to the rest of the series seems to slide by successfully, passing without comment on airing.

The first four episodes of the first season go about the way first seasons of hour-long drama series go, our studio-prescribed schedule of eight days per episode translating to enormously long shooting days. Sixteen hours is not unusual for our department and many others, who have to show up before call time for setup and leave long after wrap to make sure our mess is cleaned up and the trucks are packed and on their way. And given that there are union rules for turnaround – the period of rest time mandated between the time you finish your day and the following day's start – as the week moves on, each succeeding day has a later start. Monday's call time is typically 6:00 or 7:00 AM. By Friday, 2:00 PM or later is not unusual, meaning a 3:00, 4:00, or 5:00 AM wrap on Saturday morning, that fifth workday known with gallows humor as Fraturday. There has been increasing awareness in the film biz of the dangers of long workdays, especially in cities where high housing costs in city centers like LA and New York force crews into commutes of an hour or more each way. There have been fatal accidents. There is a lot of talk of safety from the studio execs, echoed by production people. Hotel rooms are offered at the end of long days for those who want them. But most people would rather drive home at wrap, however tired they are. On the studio and production side no one does anything to cut the hours down. Hour-long shows are allotted their eight days per episode and expected to stick to it. Making the day – shooting all the scheduled work – takes precedence over safety concerns. People wrench their backs out at the end of a long night at the end of a long week or fall asleep at the wheel and crash their cars or if lucky wake up moments after dozing off, as I recall doing at least once, having drifted wide and hit the curb right after turning onto our street.

We're a few days into shooting the fifth episode when word goes around that the heads of the New York unions have instructed the crew to walk off our set at midnight, fourteen hours after that day's call time, to protest the long shooting days. We're in a Rockland County suburb. We're ending the day with the scene of Tony Soprano spying on a witness-protected ex-mobster relaxing in a hot tub on his back deck. As midnight approaches, we are nowhere near our last shot. Ilene, realizing perhaps that this is not a bluff and not wanting the bad blood of open revolt to occur, pulls the plug, and we go home.

Their hand forced, the producers and HBO allow an extra day or two per episode for the rest of the season. The show's success as the seasons roll on allows for bigger budgets and more shooting days. In late seasons, fifteen or sixteen days per episode isn't unusual, and the final episode, which David directs, shoots for more than a month.

The scripts that first season, as they come across our desks, are better than the boilerplate basics of the typical TV show, better than what we're used to getting on the features we work on, better and more interesting than anything out there, we start to realize. Those of us who got into the business because we are movie buffs have not had much to get excited about on our jobs or even in the theaters. Current European films, once the vanguard of thorny, thoughtful, and dissident content, have mostly turned to overwrought tragedy or the fluffed-up following of affairs. The only people I know still going to the trouble to track down special stuff are my film school friends Mike R and Mike K and my childhood friend Peter Cole, a poet and translator, and his wife, Adina Hoffman, a film critic for *The Jerusalem Post*. They mention films from Iran and Asia that I won't take the time to watch for a decade. Mike R has moved on from that *Quiz Show* craft service job to location managing films himself. Mike K works with me as an assistant manager for the first *Sopranos* season alongside a smart, articulate former scout named Jason, as big a film buff as anyone with a fondness for hardcore horror films I can't stomach but that the Mikes assure me are more interesting than what Hollywood is otherwise into. Mike, Jason, and I admire the first three scripts we're handed. The writing staff is a bit in flux, with a married couple who worked with David when he ran *Northern Exposure* among the few who will last more than a couple of seasons, and someone named Frank Renzulli, who sends his scripts in from LA and sometimes flies to New York to sit on set during the shooting of his episodes. Other contributors whose names appear on scripts alongside David's don't make in-person appearances and don't get second chances. David carries the writing for the bulk of the season but mostly steers clear of the set, explaining that he doesn't want his presence to put added pressure on directors. A writer is often in the van during scouting and on set during shooting, but this is not yet mandated, as it will be later. One or another of the married writers do stand by with some regularity, and David will stroll down from the writers' offices upstairs to watch scenes when we shoot on the stage. Partway through the season the director Allen Coulter is added as a producer and floats between sets and scouts, read-throughs and tone meetings, his inclusion a result it seems of his stellar execution of the first episode he directs, the one during which the crew threatened that walk-off. It's called "College."

I remember distinctly sitting at my desk at Silvercup Studios and reading that script with simple amazement. Tony Soprano and his daughter, Meadow, played by Jamie-Lynn Sigler, on the college tour in Maine. The priest at home with Carmella. It is so good, so neat and tight and with a rare darkness that when things come back around to the Soprano house and family life carries on as usual you have to laugh, especially after Tony kills the informant. It brings you to a place you haven't gone to before. No wonder HBO asks David to have Tony back off from the killing. Thank God he knows not to listen.

Location-wise it's an episode where everything clicks. Drew University stands in for the colleges; a motel I drove past a million times growing up looks enough like New England to pass muster; and the quaint main street in Tappan, New York, stands in for small-town Maine. At the end of a prep day with the scouts back in the office and the folders stacked up, I get a call from Ilene to go down to the writers' office to see David. I tell her I'll have the folders together in a minute or two.

"Don't bother, come down now," she says.

It occurs to me then that if it's not about location folders, I could be getting fired. I can't think of anything I've done wrong but also can't think of any other reason he'd want to see me. David is the opposite of demonstrative, and it's hard not to feel that only a handful of us aren't in precarious positions. I make the walk along the narrow back hallway that connects the production office to the writers' wing, housed for the first season in an on-site apartment divided up into individual offices and a central meeting space. In the hall outside there are half a dozen folding chairs where actors auditioning for roles wait their turns, a few of them filled. Before I sit down, David's assistant opens the door and tells me to come in.

David is there with the episode's director, Ilene, and two women I don't know, sitting on chairs arranged in a half circle. David's assistant introduces me. The woman sitting next to David is Georgianne Walken, the casting director. The other woman, Georgianne's assistant, hands me a page from the script.

"Sit here," Georgianne says. She indicates a chair facing them. "Read the dean," she says.

I look at the pages, find the dean.

"Miss Soprano, come on in," I say. "Shall we talk about your future?"

I pronounce the words as if it's a phonetic exercise.

"Again," David says.

"Miss So-pra-no, come on in. Shall we talk a-bout your fu-ture?"

"Um, try saying it naturally," Georgianne says.

"Miss Soprano, come on in. Shall we talk about your future?"

"Put a little inflection in it," David says.

It is at this late moment that I understand what's up. I am auditioning. I look at the line and say it . . . somewhat naturally.

"Great," David says.

"Great," Georgianne says.

The assistant asks me for my Social Security number. Someone else tells me to see Juliette, the costume designer, when I have time.

Later I'll learn that at the end of a long casting session David couldn't bear the thought of seeing seven more actors for one line.

"Get that location guy down here," he said to the room.

It is not the last time baldness and what remains of my academic mien will bring me to mind for those sick of casting sessions.

Our first scene at Drew University is a long exterior walk-and-talk between Tony and Meadow. I watch a few takes and then head off to check the other places on campus we'll move to later, including the one where my scene, as I now think of it, will be shot at the end of the day, as it's an interior and the priority is daylight work outside. If it gets dark the electric crew can always pump light through windows. Walking across campus I spot Gandolfini sitting by himself on a bench and decide I'll formally introduce myself. "College" comes a couple of months along in the shooting of season one, but while I have stood around as conversations unfolded between him and a director or one or another of the handful of crew he's friendly with, I don't think he knows who I am, and I don't want to simply appear in front of him during rehearsal. I walk up and stand there. He's looking at his cell phone. Eventually he looks up. Says nothing.

"Hi, Jim," I say. It's what everyone calls him so I figure I'll do the same. "I'm Mark, the location manager, but it ends up I'm gonna be the dean of admissions later. In the admissions office scene."

He continues to look at me, saying nothing.

"Anyway, I thought I'd mention it," I say.

I don't know what I expect him to say. There's no real reason for him to say anything, I realize. And he doesn't, for a moment.

"Oh, okay," he finally says. "Good to know. Good luck with it."

"Thanks," I say, maybe too eagerly. "See you later."

He nods.

I walk away.

I get in my wardrobe when the second AD tells me to. I have a small room in the honeywagon, the sixty-foot-long tractor-trailer with crew bathrooms and small changing rooms for actors with one-day roles. It's a SAG rule that actors with lines have a changing room of their own. In the room I step into there's a padded bench, a short wall-mounted table with a mirror above it, a metal folding chair, and behind an accordion door, a toilet and tiny sink. Hair and makeup will check me on the set, I'm told, so I'm spared a visit to that trailer. I head over. I wait for the DP to finish lighting. When he tells the AD he'll be ready in five, Allen Coulter walks over and shows me where to start and where to land to say my line. I've known him since the crime series, where he came in to direct second unit and, succeeding at that, went on to helm half a dozen episodes. He works fast and has a fluid camera style (he may be the originator of the circular study of Tony as he makes his bathrobed trek to the bottom of the Soprano house driveway to retrieve the day's paper). He is a nice and, for the film biz, an unusually cultured man with a soft southern accent. He likes to eat well, which sometimes causes him, on scouting lunches, to choose inappropriate dishes like seafood specials in Jersey diners, about which he is occasionally teased and from which he is definitely at least once sickened. He talks for a while with Jim and Jamie-Lynn and the kid who walks by at the end of the scene, actual actors, unlike me. Then it's time to rehearse, and shoot. They start with a wide shot, Jim and Jamie-Lynn in the foreground and me appearing in the doorway in the deep background. I get the line off with about as much affect as my initial iterations in the casting session.

As they reset for the following take, I open the door to see what's up. Alex, the DP, approaches the spot where I will land and holds his fist up as if checking the light. "You know, Mark," he says, "it would be great if you could open the door only this far." He swings the door to where he'd like it to stop. He then says, "This way it won't block the light and maybe if you're thinking about that, it might make the whole thing easier for you."

I do what he says and it works. I give it a decent reading and Allen says, "Very good." Then he walks over. "Hey, why not try saying the second part of the line after Jamie-Lynn walks past you, as you're closing the door."

I do this and we move on to a medium shot and a close-up, and then it's on to coverage of the kid who walks by and coverage in the other direction, including when Jim looks up at and reads to himself the placard on the wall across from where he's sitting. It's a quotation from Nathaniel Hawthorne, an alumnus of Bowdoin, the school the scene is supposed to be taking place at:

NO MAN CAN WEAR ONE FACE
TO HIMSELF AND ANOTHER TO
THE MULTITUDE WITHOUT
FINALLY GETTING BEWILDERED
AS TO WHICH MAY BE TRUE
— HAWTHORNE

It doesn't make much sense in a college admissions office but is perfectly apt for what has just befallen Tony Soprano. The episode is commonly considered among the best of the series and of dramatic television overall. I take away $600-plus for my acting services and receive, over the decades, regular residual checks adding up to a few thousand dollars more, having deposited electronically as I write the first draft of this paragraph, mid-Covid-pandemic and twenty-plus years after my performance, one worth $2.17 after taxes.

Though the writers come and go, the directing team is to a large extent established that first year. Four directors will ultimately direct fifty-four of the eighty-six episodes, with David directing the pilot and finale and a handful of others notching three or four each. One of the regulars is John Patterson, a friend of David's from Stanford film school, who directs two episodes in season one. I met him years back on reshoots of a Dick Wolf series pilot, law-enforcement-related like everything Wolf does. John is genial and wise and has a rare quality of being greatly settled in himself, never seeming to be pushing for position or angling for a better slot or the next gig or a more prestigious TV show or movie. He served in the air force, doing something in a B-52, and was renowned in the production world for having directed the pilot of Wolf's *Law and Order*, the very first episode, that is, of the very first version of that long-running and endlessly spun-off series. He liked to say that that one job bought him his sailboat, which he keeps near LA and offers more than once over the years to take me out on. It's one of a few such invitations I regret not having taken up, not so much out of interest in being on the ocean as for John's gentle and cheerful company, his mild interest in more than simply what a person could do for him (one of his favorite expressions in regard to the entertainment world, when something untoward goes down on a scout or on set, is a droll and even apologetic, *It's a selfish business*). He's been through it all so many times he has developed production shortcuts including, when scouting a location he instantly recognizes as unworkable, announcing loudly and smilingly so everyone, including the property's owner, can hear it, "Fantastic," a signal for the location manager (me) to step up and thank whoever is showing us around, explaining that our first visits are always fast and we'll be in touch if we choose their place.

The episode after "College" is directed by Alan Taylor, an NYU alum who directed a magical thesis film shown to all incoming classes for years. He has directed a slight, amusing indie and a slew of episodic shows. He'll direct nine episodes of *The Sopranos* and squeeze in a couple of indie films off-season and then move on to two big-budget but unusually unsuccessful sequels in the sci-fi and superhero genres. He's intelligent and sensitive with a more pronouncedly polished cinematic eye than many TV directors. In manner he is fastidious and, to those impatient with careful deliberation, as episodic prep teams tend to be, fussy. In every location we scout, he finds a corner and squats, holding his hands in front of his face to look through a thumb-and-forefinger formed movie frame. I've come to believe that this mannerism is less affectation than convenience, a way to get time in a potential location away from the nonstop chatter of the scouting group, the endless hours in the van making us over-familiar and not always focused on the work we're there to do.

TV puts directors in peculiar positions. They are for the most part journeymen who go from show to show, careers cobbled together based on past performance and friendships and gaps showrunners and producers need filled. Certainly, there's the usual on-set importance of the role, but creative latitude is necessarily stymied by the dictates of writing producers, the crutches of recurring actors, and the lens, camera angle and shot-size preferences of DPs, all of whom can exercise a kind of veto power over anything innovative. Directors accustomed to features might work to alter rote reactions, requesting performance adjustments or more unusual coverage than the standard progression from wide to medium to close shots, but ambitious approaches don't easily fit within the confines of even our expanded schedule, where five or six pages are shot per day (on a feature two or three pages is common). The most crucial decisions in prep, including costume, location, and prop picks, pass through showrunners and writers, and in editorial the showrunner ultimately decides what takes get used and what beats and scenes stay or go. Returning directors develop a good sense of what David will go for and manage to inject their own inspired moments into things where they can: In Allen Coulter's case those long flowing camera moves, in Alan Taylor's an artistically arranged frame, in John Patterson's a creeping camera pushing in on an actor's face to punctuate a scene or to point out a heightened moment.

Periodically we hear in the van or sitting around on the set a director's tale of a nighttime call from David about a scene he's seen in dailies, his tone never much more than neutral and his questions along the lines of *What were you thinking when . . . ?*

He does not often hand out compliments, though he is generally generous with praise and gratitude during premiers and interviews and wrap parties.

As the seasons roll along, people maneuver for promotions or ask for new challenges. Our A-camera operator Phil is bumped up to co-DP so that the workload on Alex, who shot the pilot, becomes more reasonable. He and Phil rotate scouting and shooting, allowing for a more efficient prep and a more well-rested DP. Michael Imperioli writes a script. A post producer directs an episode as reward for good work in the first season, in particular his help with music. David prefers needle drops, as licensed music is known, to composer-created scoring, and the show's soundtrack gets high praise everywhere, but evidence suggests the post producer's directing doesn't do it for David. He isn't asked back. *Sopranos* style involves fixed or dolly-mounted camera and low and wide angles. Those who stick with the program do fine, some scoring superb entries based almost always more on the strength of the script than anything they add to a show whose look has long been set. The cast doesn't have much range once you move beyond Jim and Edie's magical mutability and the couple of costars who have similar reach and intelligence, Michael Imperioli and Drea DeMatteo, who plays Christopher's girlfriend Adriana La Cerva, among the regulars who have real range.

Enough of my friends move into directing on other shows to make me think that almost anyone with ambition and awareness who's spent time on sets can direct TV. If you can put the camera in position for proper coverage and hit the showrunner-specified script highlights, you'll end up with a usable episode. My friend Mike R, the person with the most encyclopedic knowledge of movies of anyone I know, soon forgoes the financial rewards of a production career on major studio fare to produce character-driven low-budget features.

He also writes reviews and essays, including an article for *Filmmaker Magazine* ("TV Is Not the New Film," July 23, 2015) about the episodic revolution *The Sopranos* was so central to, comparing high-end TV with feature films, concluding that for all the things great TV is, it is not cinema, and it is not cinema chiefly because it shifts creative control away from the director, placing the bulk of it on the showrunner, with remnants dispersed among a rotating round of directors, writers, DPs, actors, and others. The quotes below from his piece capture, I think, the drift of the argument:

> TV is a dialogue-driven medium. In TV, the writer is king. In series TV, writers work under the guidance of showrunners to create overall series arcs. Individual writers distinguish themselves in the crowded writers room by writing dialogue that soars and leads to a dramatic dynamic between characters that otherwise would not be present. In TV, dialogue is the most important means to communicate plot, theme and character to the viewer.
>
> TV is primarily a medium-tight format; closeups somehow feel too specific in a TV drama. But in cinema, story space allows for a greater variation in shot size and depth staging. In a story that is being told without a reliance on dialogue, those visual options become extremely significant. In cinema we can spend screen time, sometimes through an extended held shot without a cut, to access the character's inner state of mind. Getting a sense of a character's place in the world, without using dialogue, but through the presence of the camera, is what we talk about when we say "cinematic."
>
> Films that don't rely on steep dramatic arcs to sustain interest rely on other components to engage viewers,

and those other components become the essential core characteristic building blocks of the cinematic experience. In TV, the script may actually be the blueprint for the final product. In film, the script should be a starting point only; the direction needs to transcend the script in order for it to be called cinema.

The ability to tell a story visually, utilizing means other than just dialogue and plot, is the unique potential of cinema. It may be unusual for current American directors to fully exploit this potential, but if we are going to distinguish ourselves from long-form TV series then it is these qualities that we must emphasize and relish.

Not that directors don't make a difference. The core team is if not essential then at least instrumental in the show's success. Their ability to judge and capture performance and their visual flair help make the show what it is, none more so than Tim Van Patten, who is the last of the four directors to make a season one appearance and who will ultimately rack up twenty episodes, more than anyone else. He's another crime series alum, an actor from his late teens who moved into episodic directing in his early thirties and stayed there, refusing offers of further acting roles, including from producers of the crime series and from David. Warm, engaging, and funny, he makes a kind of home at HBO and has a hand in many of their big shows including *Sex and the City*, *Rome*, *The Pacific*, *Boardwalk Empire*, and *Game of Thrones*. Everyone on the crew seems happy to see his name on the upcoming directors' roster. I know I always am.

Mike K and I have worked together as manager and assistant on a feature, a pilot, a TV movie, and the New York portion of another feature. It's all gone well. I'm somewhere scouting or headed to a meeting and he's with the shooting crew in the West Village at a funeral home location when he calls to tell me the owner has overheard a rehearsal of a line to be uttered by Junior Soprano, who is played by Dominic Chianese, about the old woman in the casket having given him his first hand job. The owner has just told Mike that it's a family business and that you can't say that kind of thing about a corpse in his establishment. Mike has already voiced the crucial counterarguments: that script-wise the action is happening in New Jersey; that we won't identify the location by name; that it's fiction. The owner doesn't care, telling Mike he won't let us shoot that line in his place. I tell Mike to call Ilene, and she connects him to David, who (Mike later tells me) starts to improvise lines over the phone to use in place of the scripted one. Eventually David decides Junior should say, "She had great legs." Mike writes it down, gets off the phone, gets the owner's okay, and relays the line to the director and script supervisor, and the company continues to set up for the shot.

Before the camera rolls David calls Mike back and says, "Fuck it, either he lets Dominic say the line the way it's written or we leave."

The owner won't budge and that's that. The crew loads up the trucks and the scene does not get shot. The art department will toss up a few walls at our stage, add a bunch of flowers and a casket, and the line will stay in, adding unanticipated set costs and shooting hours. I feel somewhat at fault and make sure from then on that we're up front with location owners about the racy, racist, and sexist content in the scripts, and more than a few times the scouts are turned away from locations because of it, a far better outcome than having the whole circus show up to find out someone in position to put the brakes on has heard something they don't like and won't let us proceed.

Six months or so after we start, shooting on season one ends. During the couple weeks of wrap we get, we're asked to put together a list of possible places to drive past for an opening credit sequence that will take the viewer from city to Soprano house. We propose some repeat locations and some we know David likes the look of. Director Allen Coulter heads out with assistant manager Jason, Jim driving and Phil shooting as the Caddy makes its way up the Lincoln Tunnel helix, over to the Turnpike, across the Pulaski Skyway, and past Pizzaland, Kearny row houses, and the rest. It feels tossed together but turns out to be enduringly effective, that opening song and the cigar Jim holds doing significant work. The sole notable alteration to this opening sequence over the years will be the post-9/11 removal of a shot of the World Trade Towers seen through a sideview mirror.

5

My New Jersey Family, Part Two

I grew up in a two-story, four-bedroom tract house built in 1962 on a cul-de-sac called Eros Court, named after the Greek god of love and sex. Eros did and didn't apply to our half acre. Six years after we moved in, my mother and father split up, and my younger sister and I stayed there with our mom. It would be years before my sister started bringing boyfriends around, and though I was three years older, I was on the same calendar as her with my first couple of girlfriends. Our mother didn't wait long, though, before introducing us to Eddie, the man she broke up the marriage for, and after a series of visits that often became overnights, he moved in and lived there during a good part of the years we attended middle and high school.

He sold airplane parts and other mechanical items, describing himself as a jobber. He had two children slightly older than me, one a tall and imposing boy who played tight end on his high school football team and the other an appealing and forthright girl who, during the one afternoon I spent with her, introduced me to the Jackson Browne album *Late for the Sky* and an attitude of cool indifference toward the adult world.

Eddie was an outgoing, handsome, decent man who I later learned thought I hated him, a natural enough response to my quiet, mirthless sullenness. I may have hated him, but if so this feeling went straight from my subconscious to my face without making a stop in my conscious mind. In line with what I'd gleaned from his daughter, I didn't think much about him or my mother. They were to be avoided or spurned in favor of non-familial pursuits, which over the years shifted from football, baseball, shoplifting, and science fiction to golf, skiing, masturbation, and literary fiction, with the collection and study of rock-and-roll records bridging the divide between these two sets of suburban sports and pastimes.

Many years later I attended Eddie's funeral — he died young of cancer — and, after the service, having waited in line to speak to his son and daughter, I was so intimidated or unschooled or oblivious that I failed to offer condolences, simply saying to the son something along the lines of, "How are things going?" I wanted, I know, to have a normal check-in. He gave me a hateful and disbelieving look that instantly made me aware of my discourtesy and that in retrospect may have been banked for just such a moment, having perhaps heard from his father what a brat I'd been.

After the sale of the Eros Court house my mother and her new husband, Fred Paul, who entered the scene after Eddie exited, moved to a town house closer to the city and Fred's children. Tana and I would go there for dinners or the occasional overnight. It was a spacious place that backed on a narrow preserve, a short span of woods straddling a stream. We once saw a red fox on the back lawn.

One day my mother called and said, "The house was broken into."

"What did they take?" I asked.

"They took my jewels and furs. They didn't bother with anything else."

I asked if she or Fred left the sliding back door unlocked as they sometimes did.

"No," she said.

"No what?"

"No, we didn't leave the door unlocked. The police didn't find any signs of a break-in."

"Mom," I said. "Really?"

"What?"

"It's Fred, Mom," I said.

"Don't say that," she said.

"It's him," I said.

Fred gambled. He bet heavily on football through a bookie. Nickels or dimes, which meant $500 or $1,000 bets. He studied point spreads, put money down on over-unders, sometimes made complicated quarter or halftime or other incremental bets I didn't understand. Some Sundays I'd sit watching football with him and ask him who he had. Sometimes I overheard him on the phone with the bookie upping the stakes or hedging. He took my mother to Vegas many times. He brought me along on one trip to Nassau, Bahamas. He was the kind of player casinos courted and covered expenses for. Free plane tickets, free hotel rooms. I went to the beach, had a couple of dinners with him, spent a little time each night in the casino playing $5 or $10 blackjack, losing my allotted amount sooner or later. Then I'd find him and watch him for a bit. He played at the $50-minimum blackjack table. He used a stack of $100 chips, sometimes losing or winning a thousand bucks a hand. I don't know how he did that weekend in the Bahamas. I know in the end you always lose, and in the case of bookies, all mob-run, you are made to pay or made to suffer, so it was not a big leap to go from no signs of a break-in and missing jewels and furs to a gambler who needed to raise cash quickly or provide means for others to do so.

My father felt the same, telling my mother as soon as she told him about it that it had to be Fred. This made me happy, as I was always looking for concordance with my father, finding it rarely. We even had a laugh about it at the time.

My mother never conceded the point. Years after they divorced and after Fred Paul, too, died relatively young, a collection agency found her. There was $37,000 owed on a credit card in her name, the card long expired. Fred had gotten hold of it and run it to its limit. He'd been intercepting the bills and making interest-only payments for years. He stuck my mother with the principal. She fought it, sometimes with my help, but we couldn't get the debt dismissed. Years later the lawyer-son of her last boyfriend took care of it.

Now and then my father went to Tabatchnik's, the well-known Jewish delicatessen in an old strip mall where his father sometimes worked the counter. If he had a hearing or trial at Bergen County courthouse in Hackensack, for instance, he'd stop by on his way home. The deli was in the town my mother and Fred moved to. One day my father pulled into a parking space in the strip mall just as Fred, who had parked moments before to go to a barbershop at the same mall, opened his car door, into which my father crashed. I saw how this might be construed as a kind of fortuitous gladiatorial showdown between romantic rivals but couldn't get there myself. If it was more than sheer accident it might evidence aggression – and even attachment – on my father's part. In reality, I knew he was nothing but relieved that my mother had made a match. He was deeply committed to his second wife and confessedly happy my mother had taken a payout on our old house, putting him fully in possession of the place, which he rented out for years before selling it off. I heard that after he sold it, it burned down and was replaced by an oversized monstrosity. I never went back to check.

6

Between Seasons: An Innocent Man

Soon after wrapping season one of *The Sopranos* in 1998, an old boss, Carol, hires me to manage locations for *The Hurricane*, a feature film about boxer Rubin "Hurricane" Carter, starring Denzel Washington. The project is resonant for me for its setting in Paterson, New Jersey, where my father grew up and worked for so many years, where I spent a couple of summers working for him, and where, after I got my master's in English and years before I jumped career tracks, I taught classes at the local community college. And in a more proximate link to Carter's case, there are my family's ties to Arnold Stein, a law school friend of my father's. Arnold represented Carter's friend John Artis at the initial trial, and in a kind of mildly misguided – Arnold was on Carter's side of things, after all – but to me nonetheless admirable act of solidarity, my sister blasted Bob Dylan's then newly-released song "Hurricane" from her bedroom stereo one night when Arnold and his wife were over for dinner, letting the adults downstairs know that while they enjoyed food and freedom, Rubin was sitting, as Dylan sang, "like Buddha in a ten-foot cell / an innocent man in a living hell."

When I start work on the movie, I give Arnold a call to ask about the case, hoping I'll learn something helpful or of interest to tell someone I am working for. It has been thirty years since the trial at which Carter and Artis were convicted of murder, and more than a decade since both were released and exonerated. Now a judge in Morris County, Arnold says

he never was sure about the guilt or innocence of his client or Carter, not that it mattered in his legal role, nor did it excuse the fact that the trial was a sham. He says he retains many fond memories of his mentoring by Carter's attorney, Raymond Brown, a north Jersey legal legend for whom Arnold worked for a time and who sent Arnold many high-profile cases. Brown's clients over the years included Black Panthers, Amiri Baraka, and — what else? — corrupt New Jersey politicians including Camden mayor Angelo Errichetti of Abscam scandal fame, whose story will be a key part of a film I'll work on many years later.

The Paterson police have a firmer opinion of the Carter case than Judge Stein. Many of the senior members on the force tell me they know he is guilty, lack of evidence and undue prosecutorial pressures on witnesses notwithstanding. The warden of the stone-fortress-like rectangle called Trenton State Prison, where Carter spent many years, feels the same way. Nevertheless, he approves our filming at his prison, where we shoot some big exteriors. For interiors we go to the state prison in Rahway.

The cell block and cell where Carter is shown stewing, writing, and working out will be built on a stage in Toronto, where most of the movie will be filmed. We will also shoot for a few days in Paterson, including on the actual street and at the still-extant storefront of the Lafayette Bar and Grill, where the murders happened, thanks to the shockingly reasonable Paterson deputy police chief Jim Wittig, who supervises film shoots for the city. Jim will soon become chief and will help us a lot on *The Sopranos*. During our prep for *Hurricane*, he slips me a manila folder with copies of the three-decade-old crime scene photos, gruesomely fascinating Weegee-esque black-and-white studies of splayed bodies and ink-dark blood puddles. At one point before our permits are granted I am asked to attend a meeting in the office of Paterson mayor Martin Barnes and his communications director. We sit at a conference table outside the mayor's office and go over the details of our shooting days, after which the communications guy ducks into the mayor's office and emerges with the mayor and an architectural illustration of a youth center, which he props up on an artist's easel. The mayor expresses how fully he appreciates the assistance we will be giving the city to help construct this beautiful building. After he's gone, the communications guy hits us up for a $300,000 donation. I take this in, say I'm sure we'll give something toward this worthy project, and once outside call Carol, who laughs at their shamelessness. Ultimately a more reasonable number is arrived at – a donation of $20,000 or so on top of city-incurred expenses including police overtime and parking used for period picture cars and our working trucks. A few years later Mayor Barnes is indicted on forty counts of corruption. A *Sopranos* connection who is a big player in local politics will inform me that one of the scams the mayor profited from involved the selling of city buildings dirt cheap to developer friends who on resale siphoned chunks of the profits back to him.

The job is otherwise uneventful, thanks in large part to Carol's typically tactful steering of things. The director, Norman Jewison, a fastidious, even-keeled man, one of those directors who surrounds himself with characters rather than being one himself, is old-school in his reserved manner and his expectation of a thermos of scotch (or something similar) as the day's last shot is announced with the standard walkie-talkie transmission, "Martini's up." On a scout of Rahway, we're locked down for an hour in an upper-tier rec room during some sort of prison disturbance, in the air an edgy feeling of looming disaster until the prison guards get the all-clear. I remember during the same visit the accommodating actions of a mild-mannered prisoner when our escort asks him to step out of his cell so an art director can take measurements for use in the Toronto set build, the guard explaining as we walk away that that man committed a triple murder and was not leaving the facility, ever.

The film shoots in the New York area for a week or two before heading to Canada, the New York crew full of faces familiar to me from prior jobs. The director of photography is Roger Deakins, an often charming and always intense man without the diva-like histrionics of some top DPs, though I remember, after one scout when people at the Jersey City courthouse have pushed back about rafter access inside the historic dome over the lobby, Deakins staring across the lunch table at me and sternly stressing how essential lighting access to the dome is to the success of the scene to be shot below it, putting me on notice that he will consider it my problem if permission isn't granted. One of the trickier functions of location managing is this straddling of the line between the sealed-off world of film production and real-world concerns, producers, directors, and DPs being people used to getting their way and the world not always in accord with the idea that a film company's wishes are the most important item on any agenda. This one works out. Deakins's gaffer, Bill, who'd been at that lunch when the request was made, later laughs about it, telling me that with the number of lights Roger had his crew put up there pounding heat down on that hundred-year-old stained glass, he's surprised the mullions didn't melt and send the whole setup crashing down on the shooting crew below.

The film's female lead, Deborah Kara Unger, blond and beautiful, has a disarming way, when she catches you staring at her, of crossing her eyes and sticking out her tongue and is the most pleasant of the cast. Denzel, while distant and insulated from any approach thanks to a team including assistant, bodyguard, driver, hair, makeup, and costume people, seems to take respectfully to heart all the things Jewison has to say. He steps out of his cocoon at one point on a street in a particularly impoverished part of Paterson to talk to a small crowd gathered at a police cordon, where he signs autographs and allows photos to be snapped. We learn quickly not to ask for the usual favors from him, though. No signed headshots or handshakes with local bigwigs. The first and only time we ask, his assistant responds with a flurry of four-letter words and an instruction about where we can shove such requests, causing us to wonder if Washington's reputation as difficult doesn't have more to do with his team than himself.

As we go through the usual stages of scouting, prepping, shooting, and wrapping the New York and New Jersey portions of *The Hurricane*, my wife and I and an ever-increasing portion of the country watch the initial airing of *The Sopranos*. Just before the first episode appears, on January 10, 1999, *New York Times* critic Caryn James anticipates many reviewers, finding it to be "one of the more sustained and engaging new shows to arrive in recent months." As the episodes drop, the acclaim grows. *The Sopranos* is suddenly everywhere. The *Times* will print enough articles about it over the next year and a half to publish a book of them in June 2000. It feels like Tana and I overhear people talking about it all around us every time we go out to dinner, and this will go on for years, the show hitting its first-run peak viewership with season four's debut during the fall of 2002.

7

My *Sopranos* Years, Part Two

The thought of going back to the show for its second season engenders rare anticipation. Ilene lets me know there are some changes being made. *Not a great fit* is what's offered as explanation for more than one withheld invitation to season two. The production designer and production manager do not return. The production designer's replacement, who'd been an art director on movies I'd worked on in the past, will stick around for all of the following seasons and will move on to do the pilots and some seasons of successful shows *Sopranos* writers themselves run, post-*Sopranos*. On one of these, this deeply experienced and erudite man will get caught up in an incident resulting from the blurring of professional and personal lines that people in power often cross, when one of the longest-lasting of our writers now running his own show solicits the designer's help in decorating his new New York home. The designer is put in direct contact with the showrunner's wife, who, maybe expecting more attention or options or a different approach than the designer provides, expresses her dissatisfaction with the way things are going. The designer, complaining to a friend, calls the showrunner's wife, among other things, a *schnorrer*, a Yiddish word (meaning, more or less, "parasite"), particularly pointed perhaps as the designer is not Jewish but the wife is. He accidentally cc's her on this emailed complaint. He is not asked back for that show's second season, and though he's already in talks with David about designing his 2012 feature film *Not Fade Away*, he is dropped from that project. The designer, understandably upset by events and momentarily uncertain about his future, soon makes a full recovery, his résumé to include grand period series and Scorsese features, for one of which he gets an Academy Award nomination.

A former location manager is brought in to replace the production manager, the second season in a row someone who'd done my job a few years back has been put in above me, to my chagrin. In my department Mike K doesn't return, allowing me to promote my longtime scout and location assistant Gina to assistant manager. She deserves it and does well. She'll take over managing for me a few years later when I move up myself.

The Sopranos second season starts with a few requests from the writers' room including a location for a "bucket shop," a scam stock brokerage business the writers think will crop up often in the coming scripts. One of the scouts finds a recently vacated building on the Newark waterfront not far from the train station, we make a deal for an extended rental, and the art department takes over with paint and cubicles and temporary walls, creating a set in a spot we'll rent for a couple years and shoot at for a couple days. Sometimes what the writers have in mind as they break story for the season doesn't end up as central as expected as the scripts get turned in and the episodes get shot.

The second season is put directorially almost exclusively in the hands of Tim, Allen, and John Patterson. Lee Tamahori, who directed the very fine movie *Once Were Warriors*, solicits an episode and David accedes. During shooting it becomes clear that Tamahori is ignoring the pilot's wide-and-low-angle aesthetic for his preferred longer-lensed look. Along with a focal length preference, Tamahori arrives with a young female assistant who hops in the van with us while scouting and stays by his side on set, causing assumptions to be made and looks to be exchanged. We pay close attention when, six or so years later, during the filming of one of the last *Sopranos* seasons, news about Tamahori's arrest breaks. He has evidently offered to perform a sexual act on an undercover LA cop, for cash. Tamahori is described as having been wearing a tight dress when arrested. Among the informative insights coverage of the incident affords is that Tamahori reportedly favors latex.

Writing-wise the married couple has returned; Frank Renzulli, still sending in his scripts from LA, writes the very fine "Toodle-Fucking-Oo" episode that Tamahori directs. It includes the moment, whose truth parents of teens everywhere instantly clock, when Meadow suggests to Tony and Carmela her own virtually meaningless punishment involving the temporary withholding of her Discover credit card, giving Tony and Carmela an easy out from the tough task of teenage discipline, an area soon to be a sticking point between Tana and me and probably the toughest test of our long relationship. Renzulli also writes the similarly sharp "Happy Wanderer." Terry Winter signs on for season two and instantly contributes on-the-money stuff with Renzulli-sharp dialog and memorable background business (I remember laughing out loud when Ralphie describes as "shrapnel" the piece of toenail launched into the air by a nail clipper he is wielding). Rounding out this crew is twenty-six-year-old Harvard grad Todd Kessler, hired based on a test script he writes whose plot picks up a thread from the pilot involving Christopher's celluloid dreams. Todd will go on to run *Damages* and *Bloodline*, the latter a favorite in my house, but on *Sopranos* his road is bumpy and short. Years after his employment on the show he tells journalist Brett Martin, the writer of a book about showrunners called *Difficult Men*, about being fired right after receiving news of his nomination for an Emmy for co-writing with

David the season two finale, "Funhouse," Kessler confessing that the manipulative and demanding boss Glenn Close played in *Damages* had a bit of David in her. Martin's account gives David the last word: "When told Kessler's version, complete with its overtones of Freud and betrayal, he says drily, 'I might have had more on my mind than he did.'" Martin also reports that David told Todd he'd "lost the voice of the show." It brings up a memory of riding in the scout van with Todd and being impressed that he was reading a John Updike novel, the kind of thing you rarely see around a film production – reading period, I mean, literary or not. I mention it to Terry Winter. Terry's terse comment about his colleague's taste in literature is, "Maybe he should be reading a book about the mob instead."

Naturally enough, given the attention paid to season one, there is now a lot more interest around the shooting of the show. Reporters and TV crews make appearances. Fans show up where we shoot, especially in New Jersey. The location department gets cold calls offering properties people are sure will be of interest and rarely are. Nevertheless, on slow days we send out scouts to shoot what's available in case something comes in handy.

HBO now allows another few days of filming per episode, nine or ten in season two, a number that climbs over the years to keep up with the show's expanding character count and multiplying story lines. Everyone pretty much forfeits the ability to say no to David at this point, though sometimes someone will try, HBO usually leaving it to Ilene to voice concerns or quote costs, particularly in regard to the increasing number of road trips the writing mandates: to a lake upstate or out to LA or Las Vegas or overseas to Italy and France, the latter written in after David buys a château in the Loire Valley and begins to spend time there and in Paris, the need for international downtime possibly contributing to the increasingly long gaps between seasons: twice in its seven televised seasons the show goes through a calendar year without airing a new episode. I remember sitting in on discussions of the Paris plot, during which Ilene tells David she doesn't see HBO okaying the extra million it will cost. David gets briefly annoyed, keeps Paris in, and off we go.

Long before that, though, we pay our dues with repeated trips to Lodi, Kearny, Newark, and North Caldwell. I drive to Queens for morning meetings and back to New Jersey to scout, sometimes riding in the van with director, designer, writer, and first AD, my old claustrophobia and anxiety occasionally arising. Either it subsides on its own after ten or twenty air-gulping, fist-clenching, squirmy minutes, or I send it on its way with help of a Xanax. More and more often, I stay in my own car and meet up with everyone to look at locations, peeling off to go to set, or to Satin Dolls or the Soprano house to make increasingly costly deals. I'm more annoyed than anyone by the amounts the owners ask for but can't really blame them. It's a huge pain to have a film crew chew up your lawn, piss off your neighbors, and interrupt the normal flow of your business. After a couple of long shoot days, the novelty disappears. Money is what makes putting up with the hassle worthwhile.

With the show all over the news, I suddenly have new friends everywhere, including a curious character with a ratty office at a corrugated cardboard plant on the outskirts of Paterson. Alan L is a tiny man with a debilitating disease that keeps his fingers permanently bent and contorted and his body in a crouch. He walks with an uncomfortable-looking sideways stagger, often with the help of a cane. He loves the show. It becomes central to his life. He knows everyone in New Jersey politics and beyond. He talks to governors and mayors and congressmen and police chiefs. He will twice during season two get us last-minute access to Newark Airport through his contact at the top of the Port Authority's board of directors. I will sometimes sit in that office as he makes and takes phone calls about state police pensions and water authority issues and from friends whose kids are in jail or about to be sent there. One old friend of Alan's, Bernard Kerik, has moved on from the Passaic County Sheriff's Office to positions of power in New York City. When I first meet Alan, Kerik is head of the New York City Department of Correction. He will become, along with his booster Mayor Rudy Giuliani, a heroic figure of 9/11 and will some years later end up in jail for tax fraud, emerging after serving his term into the far-right afterlife favored by many formerly powerful ex-cons.

Alan is one of those guys who hands out dollars as tips and says, "Take it, I have a million of 'em." His favorite expression, which punctuates his patter, is, "Not for nothing." He is also an old acquaintance of the owner of our strip club. They have a kind of brotherly hatred for each other, each happy to tell me what a scumbag the other is. Alan says he remembers when Tony was a punk doing grunt work for the mob, picking up cash from bartenders for his father's poker machines. Tony tells me he doesn't even want to go into what Alan asks the girls to do when he gets them alone in one of the lap-dance rooms. I don't want to know what either of them has on the other. I do keep calling Alan for help, though — to expedite a contract wending its way through the approval process at a state or county agency or to put in a good word for us at a police department in a town we've never been to. In exchange, we start to put him in scenes at the Bada Bing, the fictionalized *Sopranos* strip club. He's around enough to become familiar to the actors and lights up when they chat with him, even getting a kick out of the fact that some of them rub his head for good luck, telling me, "Not for nothing, but I know it's 'cause I'm a cripple. I think they like me, y'know?"

I agree with him. Tony Sirico, who plays Paulie "Walnuts," might say to me, "I see the little guy's here again," knowing Alan's my contact and that Jim likes him. Jim is one of the guys who gives Alan a rub.

Alan is a fearless and bad driver. His steering wheels have handles he can grab. He has two Caddies, one usually recently involved in a fender bender and in the shop. Because of his various government appointments – to the state police pension board, to the Passaic County water commission, as deputy mayor of Paterson – he never gets tickets and does what he wants to get where he's going. He drives fast. He has police lights he turns on to drive along the shoulders of roads or the wrong way down one-way streets. He gives me a variety of sheriffs', police chiefs', and PBA cards to be used when I'm pulled over for anything, and finally gets me a vinyl-coated card from the head of the state police officers' union with a triangular yellow shield on it that has a special meaning unclear to me. I keep it in front of my driver's license so that any cop looking over my shoulder after pulling me over will see it. While working location jobs, I drive so many miles across so many towns that I can count on being pulled over a few times a year. The cops always ask, "What's that?" when they see the card. And when I hand it to them, they always ask, "How'd you get this?" I have met the president of the union several times so I can mention this man's name, and because we hire state troopers anytime we film scenes on state roads I can explain why I know him. I only get one ticket over the many years I am in possession of this card. It happens as I approach the Lincoln Tunnel from the New York side of the Hudson River. The New York City cop who stops me asks if I'm trying to bribe him by flashing that card (at this point I've gotten so confident in its effectiveness that I start to pull the card out instead of slowly slipping my fingers under it to get at my license). I'm surprised and embarrassed. I find myself in admiration of this man, silently accepting the ticket when he hands it across to me. I don't remember if it happens before or after we film the season three episode in which Tony flashes his PBA card at the honest cop played by Charles Dutton, but the two are paired in my recollection.

Alan invites me to his annual fundraiser, a dinner and auction in the service of a Paterson hospital. I bring along signed *Sopranos* DVDs, crew swag, the promise of a set visit and a role as an extra. The dinner draws the major local law enforcement brass, mayors from all around the state, and even senators and the governor on a few occasions. I meet Jon Corzine and Jim McGreevey there, Alan proudly introducing me as his friend from the show. Corzine and McGreevey, who both served as governor of New Jersey, later lose credibility due to romantic scandals, Corzine for an affair with a union official and all sorts of personal payments made for her benefit (for a house and an apartment among other things), and the married McGreevey for an affair with a man named Golan Cipel, riotously described by the *New York Times* as "an Israeli national and erstwhile poet."

The purpose of this account is personal and originates in a desire to describe the memories that, during this period, impressed themselves sufficiently upon me to become lodged in my mind and with some introspection and digging – a look at documents saved, a viewing of films and TV shows worked on – come readily to the surface, in the assumption that such naturally arising recollections retain the true impressions of their origins. I will readily admit to a hope that the public nature of the enterprises I have been associated with might add interest or value to my perspective on them. Nevertheless, I don't mean for anyone to think that I am claiming, based upon the fact that I worked on what is widely regarded as one of the best series in the history of television, personal credit. Production people, skilled as they may be at what they do, are interchangeable. What David, the writers, and the actors achieved was aided by people performing tasks others could have performed as well, myself included, and the shade of difference among the couple dozen available people per position at that time in New York means that switching one of us for another most likely wouldn't in any noticeable way improve on or detract from any given project. I have already gone over some of the changes made in staffing between the first and second seasons without any appreciable effect on later seasons of *The Sopranos*. And in truth the way writers of the show came and went and the directors rotated in and out it's not unreasonable to ask around which people the circle of necessity should be drawn. I'd nominate David, Jim, Edie, Michael, Drea, a few other cast members, a few other writers. It's interesting, and pointless, to speculate.

"College," the first great episode after the pilot, remains a relatively fresh and accessible part of my remembrances of this time not only because of its beautifully compact and transgressive script but also because, as already discussed, I was cast in a small speaking part that gave me access to the read-through and other events not normally open to a location manager. Fast-forwarding to season three, "Pine Barrens," another outstanding episode, makes a memorable impression due to Terry Winter's script's hysterical intensity, the grand comic turns of Michael Imperioli and Tony Sirico, and its direction by Steve Buscemi, famous for roles in interesting indies and edgy mainstream stuff from Quentin Tarantino and the Coen brothers. He is the kind of person I make myself available for during scouting due to a quite standard curiosity about famous people along with an interest in less mainstream movies and their directors, his very fine dive bar serenade *Trees Lounge* – a rare bar-centric success, with the major Hollywood movies *Ironweed* and *Barfly* nowhere nearly as engaging or worthwhile. I end up glad I took the time with Steve. Along with being a decent man at the helm of a great episode, he brings to direction an actor's ease with actors that is interesting to witness and that among *The Sopranos* directors only Tim can match. My time with him pays off professionally, too, in that I will get to work for him a few years down the road when he directs the first in a trilogy of English-language remakes of Dutch movies to honor Theo van Gogh, a director and distant relation of the painter, who is assassinated by a man enraged by a short film he's made.

The remake Steve directs, to continue this digression for another paragraph, is called *Interview*. It costs a million dollars, millions less than a single episode of *The Sopranos* in even the early, less expensive seasons. Bruce Weiss is the movie's American producer, a New York indie stalwart. The two of us consult on the hiring of a small crew, some of whom I bring along from the bigger-budget world and bump up because I think they are capable. They accept the low-budget job because their higher-profile roles on it will get them a step closer to a real move up on bigger jobs, same as me (it is my first line producing gig). The rest of the crew is made up of Dutch colleagues of Van Gogh brought over for the project. These include his producer, director of photography, camera operator, and script supervisor. The Dutch are uniformly tall and attractive, an edge of scorn showing when they run up against the more regulated and stratified behaviors of an American union crew. In what is almost entirely a two-hander, Sienna Miller plays the actress interviewed by a reluctant and snobbish journalist (Buscemi) who considers celebrity profiles beneath him. They act out the long battle of wills in chunks some twenty minutes at a time, shot straight through and performed, therefore, more like a play than a film. After each take, Buscemi goes to the monitor to review what happened before commencing another. It turns out well, surprisingly lively and fluid given the budget strictures and short shooting schedule. I will go with Tana to Sundance for the film's premiere, about which I remember only that on preparing to leave the house we hear our front door open and see our son step into the kitchen with a look on his face that tells us he is as surprised to find us home as we are to see him there (we are a bit late getting going, while he is supposed to be at his friend Max's for the weekend). When we ask what's up, he tells us he's getting his lacrosse stick, which makes sense as he and Max are on the high school team. He is a smart kid and a quick thinker. The next day, in Park City, my wife gets an update from our friend Janice, Max's mom. The kids showed up drunk to dinner, which means Jack had come back to our house not for a lacrosse stick but to set up for a few hours of beer pong that resulted in three giggling guys at Janice's dining-room table, one of them at some point bolting to barf in the closest bathroom.

Backtracking to Steve's *Sopranos* directing debut, "Pine Barrens" is an early and interesting example of the adverse effect of the show's popularity. We have found a park in Essex County dense and wide enough to play out the scenes where Christopher and Paulie get lost while pursuing a Russian mobster, the episode's main location. We apply for the filming permit, filling out the standard paperwork and sending it in, and begin to make the usual preparations for parking, catering, and the rest. The permits have been rubber-stamped for us for years. With approval pending, I meet a sheriff at the park and show him the areas we'd like to film and where we're hoping to stage the rest of the company. I agree on the spot to a couple of adjustments to our plan. Not long before we're scheduled to start filming, we're told the permit has been denied, and when we get through to the person who has turned us down we're told there are safety concerns as the county is holding a hunt to cull deer. Within hours, we hear from other sources a different explanation. Essex County executive James Treffinger has been quoted in the press as saying that while "everyone in America has a First Amendment right to put forth any work, no matter how obnoxious some people may find it, that does not entail the automatic right to use public property to perpetuate harmful stereotypes." Treffinger, it turns out, took his stepfather's last name at age four. He was born James Padalino. He has hopped on the Italian anti-defamation bandwagon that is targeting *The Sopranos* and getting a good deal of attention out of it. The Essex County Sheriff soon joins in, seconding Treffinger's outrage at the depiction of Italian Americans in the show.

With no time for appeals we get back in the van and hit whatever parks outside Essex County we can get to, picking a few suitable spots in Harriman State Park, which was an earlier option rejected as a bit out of easy commuting range and – more important – out of the union-dictated thirty-mile filming zone beyond which the company must pay travel time. Now it will have to do.

Further complicating things, a couple days before filming starts the region is hit by a snowstorm. As we line up snowplows to clear parking lots, Steve and writer Terry Winter scramble to figure out how to square the fact of fields full of footprints with Christopher and Paulie's getting lost and failing to find the Russian they've failed to execute. In the end I think the more deeply forested Harriman location works out better than the suburb-surrounded north Jersey park. You can't beat the scenes of the two underdressed mobsters trudging in circles through snow and shiveringly sharing ketchup packets they've found in an abandoned van in which they've taken shelter.

Treffinger, a little over a year after pushing us out of Essex County, is arrested by the FBI and pleads guilty to obstruction of justice and mail fraud. He spends about a year in federal prison.

John Patterson directs the season three finale. The assistant location manager Jason – who had been a key player in a location prank-calling phase we'd gone through during our days on the crime series, putting on voices to freak out production people on other films with stories of access-a-rides unable to get grandmothers to vital treatments due to movie-mandated traffic diversions – is back at it, this time making regular calls to the *Sopranos* propmaster, adopting a southern drawl and speaking nonstop about his precious collection of antiques and curiosities, encouraging us to rent any of a long list of unusual items and in the course of things always mentioning his prized stuffed weasel. The propmaster responds with courtesy and mild interest to the first call, impatience to the next half a dozen, and does not answer after that. This doesn't help as Jason leaves messages on the man's voicemail, continually pitching the stuffed weasel. John Patterson overhears a few of these calls as we cruise around in the scout van. At some point Jason and John develop a strategy for further exploration of the gag.

A production meeting occurs before we shoot each episode, usually scheduled on a day we're finishing up the preceding episode on the stage and held in the large room one flight up from the production office, chairs and tables laid out in a big rectangle. David, the upcoming director, whatever writer will be assigned to set, often the other on-staff writers, and the twenty-plus department heads and assistants attend. The script is covered scene by scene so that everyone is clear on what's expected. The one that ends season three, written by David and Lawrence Konner, includes scenes set in the office of a character called Major Carl Zwingli, the commander of the military school A. J. Soprano is to be sent to. When this location comes up for discussion, Patterson rattles off what he expects dressed into it: flags, diplomas, military memorabilia. He slips into this rather standard list, without slowing his delivery or modulating his affect, a request for a personal touch or two.

"Maybe some family photos," he says, "or a stuffed weasel."

Jason and I have been warned, and as Patterson plays his part we study the propmaster. He looks up in disbelief, then looks around the room to see if anyone else registers the weasel. I'm not sure what investigating he does immediately following the meeting, but in the middle of the afternoon while most of the team works in the office, Jason's desk phone rings. It's the propmaster, who tells him he's fucked with the wrong person. The next day Jason tells us that the prior night on heading out he found his parking spot empty, his car nowhere in sight. The propmaster evidently enlisted one of his assistants and, employing his car jack and four car dollies, one for each wheel, rolled Jason's car to the dark back corner of the lot, under the off-ramp for the Queensboro Bridge.

8

Making the Most of It

There are people who will tell you they don't watch TV or that while they keep up with what's airing, they aren't interested in the gossip that constantly circulates around popular entertainment or in the behind-the-scenes stuff that filters out. I never believe it. Everyone in my experience has at least a little curiosity, if only to tell you after the anecdote you've provided at their prompting that they figured as much and that's why they don't care. This is all a prelude to stating that having even a mid-level, far-from-glamorous, relatively obscure job in film will pique almost anyone's interest, and none in my experience more consistently than being the location manager of *The Sopranos*. For years after its initial airing, the show hits heights of fascination that a broadly acclaimed and wildly popular film with marquee movie stars rarely hits and, unlike a movie, is actively in production and is thus of ongoing interest as a living entity. Once it becomes known where I work, not infrequently because I say so myself but also because my friends or family are making the most of the association and happily spreading the word, people are full of questions not only in the hope that I will tell them something that will give them an edge on Monday morning during discussions of the prior night's episode but also to be in the (however distant) orbit of a show they can't get enough of. I live in New Jersey and, after our scouts make the initial forays, am one of the first faces people see when we are looking at locations, one of the first voices authorities hear when the show is seeking permission to film somewhere. I am in touch with police departments and town officials in north Jersey, lower Westchester, Rockland County, and western Long Island. I have offers to dine all over, to play golf or tennis or get a limo sent to my house to take me and my wife for a night out, to attend banquets, to talk to classes and film clubs, to share anything at all about a show people want to hear everything about. Everyone who works on the show is, I know, going through some of the same.

I, nevertheless, have during this entire period feelings of embarrassment and discontent that easily edge into bitterness as I continue endlessly, it seems to me, to work as a location manager, a position I will not fully graduate out of until I am fifty years old, a decade or so later than most of my peers. The success of *The Sopranos* and the attention that gathers around it are for a while consolation. I can at least count on enthralling some segment of the many people I meet both professionally and socially – for example, in a courtroom in Newark during jury duty when during voir dire I answer yes to the question, "Are you friendly with any law enforcement officers?" In response to the follow-up question I explain that as a location manager I am involved in booking police for things like road closures and blank gunfire supervision and then interacting with officers on set as needed. I provide the example of my recent repeat visits to this very city having led to my socializing with a couple of its supervising officers. When one of the attorneys out of curiosity asks what job I am talking about and I answer *The Sopranos*, the attorney requests permission from the judge to approach the bench for conference and, when the judge nods, this attorney motions to opposing counsel. Soon both stand beside me, leaning in along with the judge, to ask questions about the show, before all three agree that my position vis-à-vis the police allows me to be excused from serving.

All to say I get a lot of mileage out of the show, and even a boost of confidence, and begin to feel away from work, even among the professionally and artistically accomplished contacts of Tana's who form over the years the core of our friendships, a measure of my own worth. This makes me less socially shy and stiff, and ready to relate a story from the set when called for and to make myself available for questions and stories about the show when our HBO publicist has a reporter asking for an interview that David, Ilene, the writers, and the actors don't want to deal with. Locations along with costumes and production design provide good angles for fluff pieces, and over years of trial and error I gather a handful of effective anecdotes and shamelessly repeat them. The HBO publicist counts on me to not divulge upcoming plot points or voice negative opinions about colleagues, which I seem to succeed at. At least, no one on the show ever comments one way or another about anything I say. I never mention the long work hours, occasionally absent actor, periodically predatory producer. Nothing about anyone's bad behavior, no hint about the occasional internecine struggles in the writers' room, some of which I witness, a couple of times resulting in the mutely acrimonious removal of a writer or writing duo. I certainly give no hint of a staff antsy for promotion or praise or time with David or a bigger bump in pay and make no reference to one of the people near the top of the production pyramid having become twitchy and weird and hypochondriacal and often unavailable due to pressures of work or family or basic psychological makeup.

My scrapbook includes a column with quotations in *The New York Times* and a full-page profile in *GQ*. I appear in a PBS documentary and am interviewed by who knows how many newspapers in New Jersey and New York and anywhere we go anytime no one above me is up for taking the fifteen minutes to talk to someone.

On the hunt with *Sopranos* location manager **Mark Kamine**

Mark Kamine is sitting in his Volkswagen Jetta, driving through the suburbo-industrial landscape of northern New Jersey. Slipping past his rearview mirror are multiplexes and oil refineries, sports bars and motels, reed-covered stretches of quasinatural marshland. This is *Sopranos* country—and Kamine, the location manager for HBO's Mob soap, is one of the people who made it that way.

But just ask God: Creating a universe can be a pain in the ass—especially when you've got government officials busting your balls. Earlier in the week, an Essex County official announced that *The Sopranos* was no longer welcome to film on county property because of the show's negative portrayal of Italian Americans. That left Kamine in a bind, since a pivotal upcoming scene was scheduled to be shot in a county park. He's already spent several hours this morning tramping around a state park just across the border in New York, looking for a suitable replacement. Now he has to dart to Hackensack to check on a nail-salon location; then it's off to East Rutherford to meet the series' production team, including guest director Steve Buscemi.

First, though, he must drop by Satin Dolls, a club in Lodi that doubles as Bada Bing, a strip club on the show.

LOCATIONS, LOCATIONS, LOCATIONS Your key to real-life *Sopranos* landmarks

→**Bada Bing**
230 Route 17S, Lodi, NJ The back room is on a soundstage in Queens, but the exotic dancers are actually here, at a club called Satin Dolls.

→**Satriale's Pork Store**
101 Kearny Avenue, Kearny, NJ In reality, this meat-and-coffee hangout is an abandoned storefront; the production's signage, though, remains up year-round.

→**Livia Soprano's House**
55 Gould Street, Verona, NJ Tony Soprano's mother (and later his sister, Janice) filled this house with bad vibes.

→**Green Grove Retirement Home**
103 Pleasant Valley Way, West Orange, NJ Livia Soprano's temporary home and sometime Mob meeting place was filmed at the Green Hill retirement home. As Tony insists, it's "not a nursing home; it's a 'retirement community.'"

Kamine says that to be a location manager is to work as a buffer between fact and fiction—the person who protects the fantasy world of the set from the real world and vice versa. Judging from the scene at Satin Dolls, the distinction is a blurred one: It's nearly impossible to tell the difference between the locals hanging about the set, the Teamsters and the actors in costume. Kamine heads to his command center above the bar, where two of his scouts are waiting with

meticulously prepared documents in manila folders. Each contains panoramic photos of apartment buildings, taken from every conceivable angle. Kamine glances at one and nods: "Maybe that's where they drag the body."

Kamine grew up in the nearby town of Wayne and always dreamed of getting out. But, as in any good Mob story, he just kept getting pulled back in—first as a scout for *The Hurricane*, which took place in Paterson, and then for *The Sopranos*. Now he claims to appreciate North Jersey's charms. "It's 'scenically ugly,' " he says. "Not just ugly—*interestingly* ugly."

After the Newark and Hackensack meetings, Kamine meets Buscemi and the production team for lunch. The group is seated at a long table in a restaurant's wine cellar. They're consuming large plates of pasta and speaking in hushed tones. Kamine, too busy to eat, hands the manila folders to the production designer and is back on the road. By now, the landscape we pass is beginning to look like a gold mine—an endless expanse of perfectly cinematic locations just waiting to be discovered. And if, one week, Kamine and crew somehow find themselves ahead of schedule, well... "If things get really slow," he says, "we can always send someone out to find places to dump a body."—B. M.

Of the stories I drag out more than once, one involves the
gadget chain Sharper Image, not only because the story is entertaining but also because tucked into it is the self-portrait of a
wily and even manipulative (but for the benefit of the show!)
location manager, me. The store is written into the third script
in the second season, and as usual in cases when we're dealing
with a chain, we send a filming request to corporate. Typically such places have policies. Script content will matter, and
customer disruption, and sometimes money or promotional
possibilities. Sharper Image ultimately okays filming at its
Garden State Plaza store during off hours, something we can't
make work as we have to finish at the mall early enough in
the day to make a move to another location. We approach the
Brookstone branch at the same mall as an alternative and to
our shock receive a letter back not only welcoming us at any
time day or night but also including options not typically
on offer from retail corporate communications officers. In a
quote reprinted in the *Times*, the letter we're sent says, in part,
"Your show is so good, you could use one of our products to
'whack' someone and I'd still be happy (stab someone in the
eyes with a BBQ fork?)." We take the letter to David and after
a dry chuckle and a look at the photos of the store he says he
still prefers Sharper Image, that it has a more high-tech look
and an all-glass front with a better view out into the glinting
crassness of the wide mall walkway. I tell him I'll give them
another shot and then send a copy of the Brookstone letter to
our contact there, at which point they open themselves up to
us at the required time.

Away from work I put the show's popularity to my own use,
knowing my connection to *The Sopranos* is likely to interest
almost anyone. Thus, at the annual banquet of a fundraising
foundation for which my wife does design work, when I see a
familiar figure in a wheelchair alone except for an attending

friend, I walk right over. It's the painter / photographer / visual artist Chuck Close, perhaps best known for his large photorealistic portraits of himself and others, and after expressing my admiration for a show we've seen not long ago at MOMA, I segue quickly into my job and, as expected, find he is a fan, and so after answering some questions and listening happily to him explain to the person there with him who I am and the part I play, invite him to set to see some filming. He accepts with enthusiasm and in return invites me to his studio. Like the idiot I am about such things — John Patterson's offer of a sail as previously mentioned; an invitation to the mountain retreat of the émigré writer-director Kurt Siodmak, who was a friend of my LA landlady's when I was there in the early 1980s — I never take Chuck up on the studio visit, but he eventually makes his way over to Silvercup on a day we're filming a shrink scene. Jim says a quick hello, David does the same, a couple of people ask me who my guest is and how I know him, but only our DP Phil expresses what I think is the appropriate wonder, talking about his apartment's proximity to Close's studio, in which he sometimes clocks activity.

Close will end up a decade down the line in trouble for unsavory behavior, his reputation tarnished, the formerly fawning art world at arm's length, posterity as always left to judge if good work will outweigh bad deeds.

9

Between Seasons:
Preparation for an Emergency

Season four will air in the fall of 2002, rather than in the winter as seasons one and two did or in the spring, like season three. The episodes are taking longer to shoot, and David is taking an actual break between wrapping post on one season and starting the writers' room on the next, pushing back air dates, something we hear HBO isn't initially thrilled about. But the show now has a life of its own and David is its heart, and if he wants time off back in LA or in Paris and the Loire Valley, he will be allowed to take it.

The long downtime between seasons means the crew needs to find other jobs in 2001. Neri, my boss on the feature *Sleepers*, is production managing the New York portion of the sequel to *Men in Black*, a movie that will have the biggest budget of any movie in the history of the world, as its director will happily point out to me when we meet. Months later, a few days before we start shooting, the director will ask me if our equipment trucks, campers, and vans are taking up more parking than any movie that has ever shot in New York City. "Are we bigger than the Spielberg?" he will ask.

When I start the job, I'm not sure when *The Sopranos* will be back and don't much care. Popularity, acclaim, and steady work notwithstanding, the feeling among film workers is that features are more prestigious than TV shows, and if I'm not going to move up in rank on *The Sopranos*, I'm happy to move back over to movies. Work has been coming steadily to New York. No one with even a middling reputation is unemployed for long. And with Neri, it's an easy decision, because unlike most people on the rise, who tend to be hardest on the people who do the job they only recently put behind them, she hires me and leaves me alone. She doesn't want to think about locations anymore. She isn't even interested in scouting, leaving the director, producer, and production designer in my charge for most of prep.

The designer is Bo Welch, whose distinctive résumé includes *Beetlejuice*, *Edward Scissorhands*, and a bunch of Mike Nichols films. He has been nominated for Academy Awards. He is married to the great comic actress Catherine O'Hara. He turns out to be a decent guy, tranquil and droll. He, too, seems happy to skip the scouting phase, at least at first, spending most of his time in LA designing the extensive and elaborate sets on which most of the movie will be shot, leaving me with or without a local art director to traipse around with that grandeur-obsessed director, Barry Sonnenfeld, a tall man wearing, when I first meet him, a tall cowboy hat and cowboy boots despite his having grown up in Manhattan. He has a personality sized to match the hat. We go to locations he and Bo like from scouting photos or that were shot on *Men in Black*. With us is Barry's producer, Graham, gray-haired, gray-bearded, with a dry sense of humor built to withstand Barry's constant barrage of quips and complaints. Graham has been at Barry's side for years, his steady foil.

Everyone is Barry's foil. I have a new VW Jetta, small and overpowered. When it hits ten miles per hour the doors automatically lock with a solid chocking sound. Each time this happens Barry, sitting beside me in the passenger seat, hits the unlock button. We are scouting in New York City, so we are frequently crossing the ten mph threshold. Barry resolutely

unlocks the doors every time. Chock-chock. On our first scout
– me driving, Barry riding shotgun, Graham in back – the
following exchange takes place:

"Can't you do something about this, Mark?" Barry asks.

"Barry, just leave them locked," Graham says.

"I could check the owner's manual before we go out tomorrow," I say.

"Don't," Graham says.

"What if we crash and roll and he's" – Barry speaking,
pointing at me – "dead and I can't open the doors?"

"You're in the passenger seat," Graham says. "You're more
likely to die than him."

"Mark, since these things lock when you go over ten," Barry
says, "you're going to have to maintain eleven miles per hour.
You're going to have to time the lights and traffic so we don't
have to stop until we get where we're going."

He keeps the unlocking gag up. I mean, for weeks. Chock-
chock. Chock-chock.

On one of these scouting trips, on the way to the Tenement Museum on the Lower East Side or Ben's Pizza in Soho
or somewhere else from the first movie or of interest for this
one, we turn onto a street that's partly torn up, the car and us
bumping across cobblestones and old thick wood boards and
gravel and dirt, and Barry says, "Only in New York would they
call this a road."

At one point he says to me, out of nowhere, "Did you buy
the cheapest model of this car you could get?"

A day after I turn over a videocassette of streets I've shot
as possible routes for all the driving scenes, I hear Barry's
voice – "Maaaaaaaaaaark" – as he approaches my office. He
comes through the door, leans over my desk, grabs my ear,
and gently lifts his arm, in this way forcing me to stand, and
then still holding my ear he backs out of the office, me

forced along, and we move into the hallway where Graham
has been waiting, down the main corridor past the lineup
of desks and people working at them and finally reach
Barry's corner office, Graham in pursuit, clearly amused.
I'm somewhere between amused and concerned. On the way
Barry tells me he's going to show me something, and won't
answer when I ask him what, and when we get to his office
he lets go of my ear and offers me his desk chair, and when
I tell him I can stand, he insists, and then he hits PLAY on
his VCR, and up on the monitor on a stand beside his desk
comes the footage I shot with the video camera my father-
in-law bought me, one of those large ones that fits an entire
videocassette in its body. I filmed from the passenger seat
with a scout doing the driving. We drove all over Manhattan, past the Museum of Natural History, up Sixth Avenue
from 42nd Street to Radio City to Central Park South, all
around Soho, and on streets with views of and leading to the
World Trade Center. What I am now looking at on the monitor is a very sharply focused picture of the reflection-filled
interior of a windshield and side window, and the almost
fully obscured surroundings we drove through. Barry, who
before becoming a director was a director of photography
who shot breathtakingly beautiful films (among them the
Coen brothers' first, *Blood Simple*, and their third, *Miller's
Crossing*), explains that the autofocus on my video camera
was on and did its work. This means, he patiently explains,
that since almost all the scripted driving scenes take place at
night and we correctly did our scouting at night, the reflection of the lights and buildings of the city we drove through
turned the car windows into surfaces seen rather than seen
through, and further that the darkness narrowed the depth
of focus. Meaning that what he, the director of the most
expensive movie ever made, spent his valuable time looking

at and then fast-forwarding through was a lot of images of glinting car windows, interesting as an experimental video but useless as a scouting exercise.

"It's a good thing I like you, Mark," Barry says.

"I'll reshoot them," I say.

"Turn off the autofocus."

I believe my face is bright red when I return to my office.

As our start date approaches we do some scouting with producers Walter Parkes and Lori MacDonald. They are a quintessential Hollywood couple, Spielberg partners, both startlingly attractive. MacDonald seems to have emerged fully formed as a producer early in her career, pairing with Parkes to great and long-standing success. She is mostly silent. Parkes started as a writer with a few solid, successful credits early on (*WarGames, Sneakers*) before landing fixedly in the producing slot where he and his wife have been prolific. I soon find myself befuddled by the writing credits, as the script-related notes Parkes pitches at Barry seem to be a scary combination of simple-minded and wildly off the mark. Barry shouts sarcastic or flatly antithetical replies to each of Parkes's suggestions. Parkes doesn't like the ending the script calls for, set at the World Trade Center Twin Towers, which are played as large antenna-like receiving stations for alien messages that in the end morph into launch pads or landing zones or something I no longer remember, though I do remember thinking the idea was nifty. The script itself seems, like most sequels, to be a subpar repeat of whatever worked well in the originating movie. Parkes and MacDonald will blow in and out of town, keeping the pressure on Barry in person or by phone about endings and whatever else they're worried about. I'll hear some of these conversations when we're all in the van and am present when Barry takes their calls, interactions with Parkes always causing his voice to rise from its typically elevated volume and pitch.

As part of my location duties on *Men in Black II*, I scout the World Trade Center. I visit the offices of the mall owner, which has jurisdiction over areas we'll want to access. They seem more open than such entities usually are to the idea of filming, a result I surmise of the success of *Men in Black*. Their office is high up in the North Tower. I describe what might be involved and what I'd like to see. I am then escorted around, including onto the roof of 6 World Trade Center, which presents a dynamically graphic view of the plaza and the bases of the Twin Towers. After one of our first days of filming, Barry drives down from midtown to scout the plaza himself. By this time he has sided with his producers' opinion that the ending is not ready, that the movie will shoot out what it can in New York now, travel to LA for its numerous months of stage work, and then later in the year come back to shoot an ending still to be argued over and then written. I am waiting at the curb on Church Street to walk Barry and key crew over to the center of the plaza and wherever else he wants to go, a World Trade contact available if we want to get onto a rooftop or somewhere else not publicly accessible. Barry carries a big red party cup and hands it to me and tells me to help myself. This is where I learn his wrap drink is vodka on ice. I thank him. Neri, also offered a sip, tells Barry she has a cold and wonders if sharing his cup and even drinking is a good idea. He tells her it is a very good idea.

The night we shoot outside the Museum of Natural History, I remember getting a look at the monitor and being struck by the image, park bench centered in the foreground, glass-fronted façade of the planetarium in the distance behind it.

In the scene, Will Smith drops from the sky onto the bench. Smith will be harnessed and connected to a wire run up to a crane that hangs above the bench and is rigged in a way to allow him to relaxedly land in a seated position. I have tried over my years of scouting to develop my visual skills. I have heard the word *depth* spoken by directors, DPs, and designers enough to understand that this is a good thing, having noted the tendency of DPs and operators to position actors in a way that allows walls, fences, curbs, or anything we think of as straight to cut the frame at an angle that will accentuate an illusion of three dimensions. As far back as *Quiz Show*, during the exhaustive search for a row house apartment in which John Turturro's character, Herbie Stempel, was to live, I heard the DP state more than once, as he paged through another half a dozen unsatisfactory location folders, that the narrowness and regularity of the standard three ground-floor rooms in outer-borough row houses held little visual interest, and I understood when the choice was finally made that the slightly less symmetrical progression of rooms in the chosen apartment lent it at least a dash of extra depth. The shot that Barry has lined up – Barry lines up all his shots, often specifying the lens he wants to use – gives me an early experience of spotting another sort of visual beauty in a camera frame, because in this case the bench is dead center, Smith's stand-in seated camera right of center, the brightly lit wall of glass deep in the background, the dark night filling the sky over the structure. The museum is beautiful, certainly, but it's not really featured. The shot doesn't track or pan or tilt. It sits there. Smith will land then smoothly slide over, the camera remaining static, and another actor will also drop as if from the sky exactly into the seat Smith first landed in, the kind of witty foreknowledge his character exhibited in the first film and does so once again in the sequel to the point of diminishing returns. The shot, though, via some combination of lens and light and substance, will provide a pleasing moment. Not a lot of directors have the visual literacy to do this, I think.

Late that night I am called to set by Artist, the first assistant director, and this is as good a time as any for further thoughts on this vital moviemaking role performed by uniformly intelligent, driven, and sometimes loudly punitive people, the most ambitious of whom see it as a kind of directorial apprenticeship and go on to distinguished directing careers, helped along by the more generous directors, I like to think, since some of my favorites have mentored by example or intention ADs who became quite fine directors themselves: Jean Renoir, for example, whose ADs included Jacques Becker and even briefly Satyajit Ray, and Robert Altman, whom Alan Rudolph assisted before accomplishing his odd and interesting oeuvre. There may be no better position from which to study for the directing chair than being an AD, as these people lay out the schedule with an eye to production concerns, story order, and actors' emotional arcs. They then walk their directors through the plan for each day's work, getting their sign-off. They spend most of their prep time and every minute of the shoot at the director's side, planning and often sitting in on and contributing production-side and even offering creative opinions to whatever comes in front of the director. They are usually present for shot-listing and storyboarding, for costume, set dressing, and prop reviews, and for all the other script-specific planning that might include calling for a picture car to be brought in early to allow the DP and director to sit inside with a viewfinder to pick camera angles, reviewing stunt coordinator videos of proposed fight sequences, and asking special-effects teams to tape explosion tests or car flips for evaluation. On set, first ADs are on their feet all day calling for actors and makeup checks and wardrobe changes, warning with raised voice *fire in the hole* when a gun is going to go off, or whispering into a walkie-talkie *now* when an actor waiting just off camera should open a door or climb through a window or emerge from a closet. Firsts often have back problems, bad knees, shortened life spans. When they have history with a director, they are among the initial group – along with DPs and production designers – that a producer will be told to hire once a project gets greenlit.

Artist, *Men in Black II*'s first, hasn't worked with Barry until now. He jumped in the scout van one morning a few months before we started shooting for what Barry told him was going to be a rolling interview, and by the end of the morning he was hired. He has the standard direct manner of those in this job, telling me at lunch on the first day of shooting that, aware of Tommy Lee Jones's reputation for crankiness and impatience, he went into the hair and makeup trailer when he knew Jones would be there.

"I told him," Artist tells me, "that I've heard about you so I know where you're coming from and I'm not going to call you to set until we're ready to shoot and when I do I expect you'll get right to us so we can all get off the clock as early as possible. 'Be ready when you call me' is what he said back to me. And I said, 'Don't you worry.' And so far so good."

At one point Barry says, as explanation for Jones's crankiness and bad temper, "You'd act like an asshole, too, if you woke up every day with a splitting headache from last night's drinking and you'd get surly and impatient every afternoon when you're itching to get the next night's drinking going."

When I find Artist on set that night at the museum he's in the middle of relaying instructions about the next setup to the crew, telling the tech departments their carts need to move, telling the stunt coordinator he needs to come back to camera ASAP, telling base camp that first team has half an hour. He finishes, lowers the walkie, and points at video village, where Barry sits in a director's chair, Graham standing in front of him, his back to me. "Barry's having a problem," Artist says. "You better see what's going on."

"Hey, what's up?" I ask when I get there.

"Barry is feeling shooting pains down his left arm," Graham says.

"Maybe I'm having a heart attack?" Barry says. "That's a heart attack thing, right?"

"I don't know," I say. Then I tell Graham I'll be right back.

I talk to one of the cops on our set. The cop gets on his walkie and then tells me Barry should go to the emergency room at Bellevue, that he has called an ambulance. Barry, I find out, would rather have his driver take him, so I tell the cop to call off the ambulance. I'm not sure why we're sent to Bellevue from the Upper West Side, but while they're figuring out what to do about the last few shots of the night and getting Barry's car over to set, I jog to my car and drive down ahead of them in the hope of reducing his wait time when he arrives. I talk to the admitting nurse, who seems to get it, then I meet Barry on First Avenue and walk him in. He is amazingly himself in the middle of all this, telling me in his loud voice as we walk into the emergency room that it's so nice of me to come all this way for him, that maybe I'm not as much of an ass as he thought I was. After an EKG, blood work, and monitoring, we learn it is not a heart issue. The diagnosis is stress. Days later I will hear Barry put forth the opinion that one producer's incessant nitpicking about the dailies and the script and everything else has caused him to have an almost-heart-attack, and how shitty is that? My well-educated guess is he means Parkes.

The next night we are shooting on Sixth Avenue across from Radio City. Barry seems fine. The cameras have been positioned, and Artist has called the actors to set. We hear a siren, and a moment later an ambulance pulls up to the curb lane right beside the dolly track, camera crew, supporting actors, and extras already in position. The doors at the back of the ambulance swing open and Will Smith hops out.

"Figured I'd have this here for you in case, Barry," Smith says, smiling.

10

My *Sopranos* Years, Part Three

My payroll report for the third quarter of 2001 shows two weeks on *Men in Black II*. I remember at some point getting back in touch with the World Trade Center, where Graham has told me they still want to shoot the film's finale. And I remember very clearly that I've jumped over to *The Sopranos* by no later than September 10, 2001, a Monday, as on the following morning I am on my way to Silvercup Studios in Long Island City when the attacks begin. (Weeks before that I informed Graham or Neri that I was no longer available to finish *MIBII*).

I'm crossing midtown on the way to the Queensboro Bridge listening like usual to the traffic and weather report on WINS radio when a reporter delivers news that an aircraft — it looked like a smaller plane, the reporter says — has hit one of the towers at the World Trade Center. Aircraft accidents in the city are unusual but not unheard of. Two helicopter crashes resulted in fatalities during my time in and around the city, and a few more will occur after 9/11, including the 2006 crash into an Upper East Side building of a small plane being piloted by a New York Yankees pitcher with his flight instructor on board. Once I get to Silvercup, I stand in one of the city-facing offices with the few others who have already started work on season four, looking southwest at the dark clot of smoke angling off the North Tower. I have, since getting that first report on WINS, checked in with Tana, who is driving into the city for an appointment. When the second plane hits the second tower, I call her and we agree she should turn around. She gets off at the last exit before the final descent of the helix to the Lincoln Tunnel's entrance, safely out of the crawling traffic. At the office we talk about when to call off work. David and the writers are down the hall, having started some weeks back plotting out the season and working on scripts for the first few episodes. I see an assistant accountant crying as we look out at the smoking towers. At some point, before the call is made to send everyone home, I decide to leave. I am in my car not far from Silvercup on my way to the Queensboro Bridge when I learn that the North Tower has collapsed and that the inward-bound lanes at all bridges and tunnels leading into Manhattan have been closed.

I call Tana, who is now back home watching the news. We discuss whether it's better for me to take the Brooklyn-Queens Expressway to the Verrazano Bridge and cross Staten Island from there or to head east to the Whitestone and across the Bronx where I can move farther north if the outbound George Washington Bridge gets shut down. Tana tells me that I need to get home, whatever it takes. That our family needs to be together.

I am on the roadway leading to the Whitestone Bridge when I hear on the radio that it has been closed. I get over to the shoulder and drive along it and over a curb up onto the grass to catch the last off-ramp in Queens. I follow the surface roads through Whitestone, heading for the Throgs Neck Bridge when I hear that it, too, is closed. I hear a report of the Pentagon crash. I hear that Flight 93 has crashed in a field in western Pennsylvania. I hear that there are evacuations of tall buildings across the country. That all civilian flights over the United States have been ordered to land, all international flights have been diverted to other countries, and no flights except military or government-authorized ones are being allowed to take off. The president is in the air somewhere, on the ground somewhere, in the air somewhere. Soon there are rumors of plane crashes and bombs exploding in other places – Capitol Hill, the Washington Mall, the State Department – none of which are true.

Tana tells me Jack is still in school, that they are keeping kids there for the parents who only have care arranged at dismissal-time. She suggests taking the car ferry from Port Jefferson to Connecticut and driving home that way. I call the ferry authority as I make my way east, but when they finally answer I am told I won't get anywhere near the docks, that the police are closing street access to all but town residents. I call Tana back. She decides to call the Orient Point ferry company to see if she can get a booking from that easternmost Long Island embarkation point, and she does, on the 6:00 PM boat. I call Phil, our Bellport-based summer-rental landlord, to see if he's okay with me stopping there while I'm waiting to make the drive to the end of Long Island, since I'll have three or four hours before I need to head out. No problem at all, he tells me. I call my doctor for one of many Xanax prescriptions, I imagine, he writes that day, which I pick up at the pharmacy in Bellport. I stop for cash, too, as there are rumors of ATMs shutting down. There are also fears that cell phone systems will be overloaded and that banking and phone systems are vulnerable to attack. I stop for sandwiches for Phil, his wife, and me. There are reports of people already going to stores to hoard groceries, filling bathtubs with water in case the reservoir systems are being poisoned. I hear later that David, Ilene, the writers, and their assistants walked back to Manhattan across the car-cleared Queensboro Bridge, David having signed out a large amount of cash from the accounting safe to take with him, in case.

In Bellport we eat lunch and watch the news, with its repeated airings of the smoking towers, the clouded collapses, the horrible reports of stranded and jumping and crushed people. The emergency rooms all over Manhattan have called in staff to care for the injured. But there aren't many injuries. Mostly people walked or ran out without serious injury, or died.

Eventually I leave Bellport, driving north and east. About half a mile from the ferry terminal I pull onto the shoulder at the end of a long line of cars. I am an hour early. I call Tana again. She suggests I head to the ticket office and find out what's up, since I have a reservation. I turn off my car, get out, and walk along the line of cars.

Soon I hear someone shout, "Kamine!"

It's a film industry parking coordinator I know. He walks over to me and we shake hands. He explains he was waiting for trucks to show up that morning in Brooklyn when it started and by the time he felt he could leave for home, also in New Jersey, the Verrazano wasn't an option, so like me he slowly made his way out to the northeastern tip of Long Island to catch the ferry.

At the ticket office I'm told I can pull up to the short line for ticketholders on terminal property. Soon I'm driving into the belly of the ship. I park and head upstairs. I stand on the deck as the ferry launches and stay there for most of the ride. I remember the odd calm of the beautifully clear and smooth crossing, the sky darkening, the stars out, the lights of New London appearing, all of it an illusion of tranquillity. I make the long drive down a Connecticut Turnpike almost empty of cars. I pass a convoy of military vehicles. It is after 11:00 PM when I get home. We are relieved, and on edge, and the onslaught of news over the next weeks (prep on season four has been postponed), the aircraft-free sky, the sight a week later from a park on a high ridge at the southern end of our town of the still-smoking nexus of the attacks twelve miles in the distance, induces a low-level anxiety that steadily deprives me of a deep breath. I stop watching much news, though Tana can't take her eyes off the round-the-clock reports. Almost five years later while driving across western Massachusetts on vacation, with Jack away on a teen-travel trip, Tana and I listen to the audiobook of Richard Clarke's *Against All Enemies*, and it induces in me the same breathless anxiety I experienced for many weeks after 9/11. I switch the recording off periodically to give myself respite from the book's ungentle reminder of that day and its aftermath.

It has occurred to me over the years that my having passed respectively right beside and a few miles away from the 1993 and 2001 attacks on the World Trade Center while in a car ties me in some semi-proximate way to issues that could be considered the genesis of these attacks – the worldwide but dominantly Western and overarchingly American pursuit of an enduringly cheap and ready supply of oil – and that I am participating in a growing environmental crisis and acquiescing to the heedless support of governments that are without exception oligarchic or dictatorial, kleptocratic, given to the squelching of freedoms, and, in some cases, when challenged in any way that threatens their power or fortune, practitioners of torture and murder. And while people are on the one hand making and, you could say, stealing fortunes and thereby living like kings, sheiks, dictators, industrial titans, and oil barons, and on the other hand getting persecuted and locked up for trying to exercise freedoms we in the West take for granted, we, with our historically reasonably priced gasoline and ever-larger automobiles, don't give a fuck. I didn't think about it before 9/11. And while I think about it more and more often, particularly when for whatever reason stories about fossil fuels appear in the news, almost constantly lately with rising temperatures and seas, I also, when on a job in the USA, continue my solo commutes, filling and refilling cars with gasoline. It's now twenty-plus years down the road.

Sometime in October 2001 we get back to work. Season four will reach the largest contemporaneous audience of all the show's seasons, as previously mentioned. When shooting on location, particularly in New Jersey, we have devoted fans who track us down and line up as close to us as the police we hire will allow, shouting at the actors for pictures and autographs. We have a steady stream of visitors to set, local politicians, journalists, family and friends of cast and crew, and location owners and local hotshots. The owner of the Belleville funeral home that becomes our house funeral home asks me if David wants to talk to a north Jersey mob boss who has expressed willingness to break omerta to consult on the show. When I mention it, David nervously wonders if refusing, and he auto-matically refuses such offers, will offend this person. I tell him I'll feed the usual intellectual property line to the funeral home's owner and, if need be, will talk to the guy myself. It never comes to that.

The Soprano house owners have started to look at our shoot days there as a good reason to throw parties for their friends, who will come from all over for the opportunity to observe Jim, Edie, Jamie-Lynn, Robert Iler (who plays Meadow's brother, A. J.) and whatever cast members make an appearance. They drink a lot. They get loud. More than once someone falls down and is whisked away by a spouse. It's the location department's task to keep them quiet when we are rehearsing or rolling and to keep them away from the actors to whatever extent possible, because like people everywhere they are avid for that contact. A few years later, when Jim is at his most dissolute, missing some shoot days and showing up hungover on others, he will come into the house for a moment to get away from the crowd outside. The owner begins talking familiarly to him. This is five seasons in. Jim has been to the house dozens of times, had many conversations with the man standing in front of him. This time Jim interrupts him to say, with more than a little regret, "I'm really sorry, but my memory's kinda shot and I don't remember, who are you?" The owner looks hurt. I'm shocked. I don't expect Jim to know names but to have no clue who the owner of the Soprano house is gives me a glimpse into the extent of his personal struggles.

Years of filming in one place will exacerbate any grievances in a neighborhood, will bring forth not only the starstruck but also the kooks and litigious. We don't have such problems on the Soprano house block. The residents are more than reasonable. We want to keep it that way. We don't know how long this show will run. We give out restaurant gift certificates at the end of seasons. On shoot days we pay small fees to everyone living nearby and funnel bigger checks to backyard and next-door neighbors for the repeated rolling-up of fences for cable runs, equipment storage, driveway parking, and general commotion. I get to know the touchingly warm couple in the house right beside the Soprano house. At the end of the day I sometimes have drinks there. Once the husband encourages me to take his brand-new Corvette for a spin, which I do, despite a genuine lack of interest, to not be offensive (coming back I bottom it out on the apron of his driveway and sheepishly, silently hand back the keys, hoping I haven't done any damage).

I stop at the next house over, the one that the Soprano house faces across the cul-de-sac. We will periodically request the owners leave lights on for added depth in night shots or even to be allowed to place a movie light inside for extra illumination. The house they live in, fully renovated not long ago, had momentary infamy when in 1994 – the day Tana and I moved with Jack to New Jersey – its previous owner was killed by a bomb sent by the Unabomber, Ted Kaczynski. The wife, normally happy to chat, seems distressed and rushed. I quickly fill her in on what's coming up on our filming day, including a shot of Jim as usual lumbering down the driveway for the newspaper during which we'll want full control of the street. She tells me she's sure we'll be respectful but has to get going as she is due at her sister's. She's been spending time there every day. The sister's husband died in the World Trade Center attacks.

The events of 9/11 remain in the forefront of everyone's thoughts all year, or so it seems. Its color-coded alert system is part of each day's news, and steady stories about theoretical targets are commonplace. In December the Shoe Bomber incident occurs, Richard Reid's failed and rather risible attempt to blow up a plane mid-flight not providing anything like comfort. I think of the possibility of an attack every time I cross a bridge or enter a tunnel, or go to a mall, and almost ceaselessly on my first post-9/11 plane trip in November for a friend's wedding, studying fellow passengers for signs of anger or furtiveness. In the van on a scout at some point late in the season I watch as the next episode's director, sitting per director protocol in the front passenger seat, gets out his phone and makes a call and tells his wife he is in the Lincoln Tunnel and he loves her very much and to please tell their daughter the same, the implication being that terrorists might, while we are under the river, detonate an explosive that will bring the cement and mud and water above crashing down. It is both touching and embarrassing to hear this anxiety and emotion voiced.

The episodes we shoot this season have content related to horses not terrorism. This may be because the story has already been broken — the writers have in large part outlined the season — by the time 9/11 happens, or because David and the writers have decided it's too soon to address the event, so that once we return from the monthlong shutdown following the attacks, the story lines remain more intact than our psyches and city. The recent nonfiction bestseller *Seabiscuit* seems to be a contributing factor in the sudden *Sopranos* interest in horses, the book brought up more than once by the writers. In the most horse-centric episode, "Pie-o-My," Ralphie, played by Joe Pantoliano, buys a thoroughbred that Tony falls for more fully than he does for any of the mistresses that come and go over the scripted seasons. During the prep for the episode one of the writers talks about the importance of having a goat in the stable for the scenes with our racehorse, as goats and other small animals often live and travel with high-strung thoroughbreds, on whom they have a soothing effect. Though I'm not interested enough to read *Seabiscuit*, I get a big kick out of this piece of knowledge and observe with great amusement the real-life proof of this thesis when we do bring a goat and horse together for our stable scenes. In later years I consider it clever when I designate as "their goat" the people certain high-strung cast and crew members insist on traveling with when on location, actors needing their assistant or trainer or acting coach, costume designers their assistant designer, DPs their camera operator or digital imaging technician (DIT). I love explaining, when my comment *Oh that's their goat* draws confused looks, the derivation of the trope. It's one of a number of self-originated jokes I keep on hand that I get a bigger kick out of than anyone I tell them to.

I remain the location manager during season four. The location department is well seasoned now and runs fine, whatever I am doing. I can go to set, join a director scout, sit in the office and make deals over the phone, or detour up to Bedford for a weekday visit to the therapist I have started seeing. I have long expressed interest in going back and tackling a little more head-on my muted but ongoing anxiety and occasional panic attacks, the latter having principally restricted themselves to highway driving and attendance at live theater. The shrink is a Jewish Princeton-educated Buddhist who uncannily has the same name as the first psychiatrist I ever saw, sometimes requiring in our sessions my using a locution along the lines of, "This was when I was seeing the first . . . ," always voiced with embarrassment, as if I am responsible for the coincidence. Which ultimately, though it was Tana's shrink who gave me the name, I guess I am.

I still deal with the strip club and the Soprano house. The other steady contribution I feel I make to locations at this point in my tenure comes in the initial period of scouting after we get new scripts. I am full of suggestions about the best towns to head to for new locations, as I feel I still know New Jersey better than everyone in the department except for Gina, who also grew up there and who is back for her third year as assistant manager. I imagine she and the scouts wonder when I'll stop interfering, as everyone has by now spent years driving around north Jersey and has their own ideas about what will work, but because I'm the boss one of them will be obliged to follow my suggestions rather than starting where experience would otherwise lead.

I don't know how strongly my impatience with the rut I feel I'm in comes across, but at least Ilene seems aware of it, finally letting me production manage an episode when a producer is given an episode to direct. It's for "Pie-o-My," part of which is filmed in south Jersey at the stately half-century-old Monmouth Park. The former location manager brought on for the second season as an additional production manager gives me welcome and generous advice on checking call sheets and time cards. I am also given copies of both parts of the budget, one called the amort, which details the season's fixed costs, the other known as the pattern, a template of target costs per individual episode. During prep, department budgets come in and I relay information to the head accountant about adjustments needed to the pattern due to the specifics of the current script, our job to get them to balance out by going back to department heads if it's all coming in too high. While studying these new documents and executing these new functions, I also spend time learning where to procure horses and goats, what their transport and care will cost, and for how long we can expect the actors to be able to work near them. And in addition, because Ralphie's horse gets sick in the script, I learn about the difficulty and risks involved in training a horse to lie down for camera, since it's something they don't typically do unless they're actually sick.

We stay overnight near Monmouth Park when we film there. The night before we shoot the stables, I am at the hotel bar when the crew member closest to Jim asks if I want to go down to Atlantic City with Jim and a few others. It's over an hour away. I decline. The next morning, I'm not surprised when Jim cannot be roused. I follow steps I've seen taken before by others, getting on the phone with Ilene to give her the news, getting on the phone with the teamster co-captain for updates from Jim's driver. Jim is up and moving around, Jim is in the shower, Jim is getting in the van. Jim, in this instance, will not flake off entirely but will be four or so hours late. Director, DP, cast, and crew have done the first shots at the stables by lining up the camera over the shoulder of his stand-in, shooting coverage of the other actors saying their lines and reacting to the script supervisor's readings of Jim's lines. When Jim shows, we have two cameras ready for his medium and close shots, cameras that have been set for nearly an hour as we've run out of work without him, and after we accomplish those shots we drop back for wider coverage. We get through the day with an extra hour and a half of shooting but without falling behind, Jim cursing his way through his half-learned lines, doing take after take, drinking coffees and bottles of water, alternately sheepish and churlish, the way he always is when he fucks up.

11

My New Jersey Family, Part Three

I have an image of my father showing up at the Tick Tock Diner in Clifton, New Jersey, wearing the almost brand-new and, at that moment of the show's peak popularity, magnetic *Sopranos* baseball jacket we've received as a crew gift. Out of some clearly false sense of modesty, as I readily mention my connection to the show at all opportunities, or an equally false idea of not wanting to be endlessly approached, even though I happily launch into my store of anecdotes whenever asked about the show, I instantly gave the jacket to my father, who is an avid fan of the show, keeps current with my *Sopranos*-related activities, and readily relays what I tell him to his *Sopranos*-loving circle of friends. I am happy to share *Sopranos* lore and swag with him, easy exchanges after having lived through years of staccato and uncomfortable conversations, typically sports-, restaurant-, or travel-related. We have become close enough for me to figure he might be open to talking about his experience in the war and as a young lawyer, telling him when I ask to meet that I'm thinking about using the information in short stories, which he knows I write and occasionally publish, though since a run of them in the 1980s my publishing pace has slowed to one story per decade, my film career absorbing the majority of my waking hours with book reviewing taking up most of my limited writing time, weekends needing to be measured out among family, friends, and whatever writing I have in mind.

"You like it," I say about the jacket as my father sits down.

"I love it," he says. "I wear it everywhere. I get asked about it wherever we go. I've had people offer to buy it off my back."

The conversation is genial and flows easily. I ask him about his college years, his Korean tour, his early work. Some of what he tells me I've heard before. I've heard about the UC Boulder baseball coach who asked him, once he learned that my father had a science lab that would conflict with the next day's practice, whether he was at school to play baseball or to go to classes. I know that his first job out of law school was as counsel for an insurance company. Now he tells me about the rapidity with which he learned to evaluate and settle cases, trials being the last thing the company wanted, his colleagues and bosses unhappy with him when he got stuck in south Jersey trying a case that took a full week to finish, cutting severely into the claims he could handle. He tells me about the coincidences that led to his getting off the front lines in Korea, beginning when, on a train taking him and hundreds of other soldiers cross-country to transport ships in San Francisco, an officer entered the second-class car and called out for anyone with bridge-playing skills, as he and two fellow officers up front needed a fourth. My father, who picked up the game in college, played well enough to make an impression that got him recognized many months later in a mess hall during the week his platoon was back at base for R&R. Once again in need of a fourth, this time for his tenure there, the officer arranged for my father's reassignment to HQ, where he played bridge, played in the band and on the traveling baseball team, and spent days working on a newsletter that was the local version of the army newspaper *Stars and Stripes*. The newsletter's editor was a big reader and started to pass books my father's way, and soon he was entranced, occasioning I think the cummings-ish quirks, like lack of capitalization, of pen-pal letters to his future bride, my mother, their acquaintanceship commenc-

24 february 1954 wednesday

dearest rhoda,

last letter i received form your illustrious and well-intending suite-mate
contained one (1) plea for a tall, handsome, rich, and jewish boy who might
write. well, im not tall, not hansome, not rich, but behold i am jewish.
therefore, as the story goes, i shall write. but marcia g. shall never know.
notice how cleverly i have used an alias on the front return address. am
finding it hard to xxxxconcentrate. big argument going on tonight. over nothing
as usual. seriously though, have screened the regiment in an attempt to
find witty, amusing pen-pals for everthing, er everybody that is, definate dearth
of material. anyway after you send me a few pertinent facts such as your height
widthwise(fathom that out) and a full length picture together with a beaver
freshman beannie, i will be glad to make available to you arch's"we find 'em
you keep 'em" pen pal service. if you find this letter rather short, it is.

                     i remain
                     arch
                     unfortunately

p.s. do not be offended by my gaucherie. excellent example of abortive writing.
a miscarriage, that is. write for a newspaper over here and sometimes i become
enhanced with my own ability with is actually negative minus. if you understand
this translate it and send it back.

                     again

ing while he was in Korea and remaining for his entire tour
and a few months after that strictly epistolary. This newfound
love of reading also turned his academic interest away from
science. After his service, he applied to law school.

———

I went to law school myself, the same one my father attended, Rutgers, Newark. When I was accepted and said I'd be going, his pleasure was evident, but I suspected, based on what he said to me that day – "You'll always be able to earn a living once you have that sheepskin" – it had as much to do with relief that he'd no longer have to worry about me financially as about paternal pride in an offspring's affirmation of his profession. He has had reason to worry, as the use to which I'd put the Ivy League education he'd paid for involved at that time living for free in a New York apartment in exchange for working as the building's superintendent, picking up paltry part-time pay teaching freshman comp at local state colleges, and supplementing that with a couple days a week as an administrative assistant at an Upper East Side art gallery.

I lasted a semester in law school, had a breakdown that induced extreme anxiety and agoraphobia and sent me crashing into analysis for a few helpful months until my father, calling me into his office not long after I was back up and around, pushed the bills across his desk at me and told me he would not pay them. He was many years into a second marriage, with a young daughter to look out for, and was done funding my unfathomable choices. While it was a harsh moment, and one I resented for a long time, it worked out for both of us in that I did eventually figure out how to support myself in a manner I could live with. The career I fashioned in the end and the interest my father took in it, most pronouncedly in my *Sopranos* years, reclaimed for me, and I think for him, too, some of what we had lost.

12

My *Sopranos* Years, Part Four

A trainer stands in the backyard of the Soprano house holding a leash with a black bear on the end of it. A veterinarian who is an expert marksman is nearby, the rifle he holds loaded with a tranquilizer dart. I am the one who will give him the signal to fire if in my opinion the actors or crew are in danger. I have been told by the vet that a dart loaded with enough tranquilizer to quickly stop a bear can certainly kill it if it strikes too close to the heart or in the eye or in the throat. It can also fail to work.

The bear has been brought out early to get acclimatized to the location and the pre-shoot activity. It has a silly, harmless-sounding name that I can't recall. Bubbles, maybe? People are chatting, equipment is being wheeled or carried around from the stakebeds being unloaded out front. Troy, one of the set dressers, comes through the breezeway between the new wing and the main house. He's wearing a brown or khaki Carhartt overall, and who knows what the bear mistakes him for, but it's clearly something it is not willing to confront, because suddenly it takes off, yanking the leash out of the trainer's hand, smashing through plantings that fringe the lawn, and climbing up a tree. This happens in a flash. I am in awe of the bear's speed. Others are, too, it seems, given all the *holy shits* and *did you see thats* going around. I doubt, if the bear had headed toward Troy or anyone else on the crew, that I would have given the vet the signal to shoot in time, and even if he decided on his own, I can't imagine he would've raised the rifle quickly enough to take the shot.

The trainer coaxes the bear down from the tree, gets it back in position. We get into the scenes. At some point, Jim brings his four-year-old son over for photos. The trainer is accommodating. I watch from a distance, eyeing the bear and the vet, not happy.

I am fully half-promoted for this fifth season and will receive credit as an assistant unit production manager, a non-position that I will share with one of the second assistant directors and the head of the office staff. I'm half happy with this half measure, and fully happy to finally promote Gina to location manager, which she has more than earned. The threefold thickening in the production middle gives our production-side producer and UPM the ability to come and go, to not work as many late nights and Fraturdays. I get a little more money. Occasionally I am given a share of a full UPM credit and the reward of the eventual residuals that go along with that credit, which will over the next twenty years add a few thousand dollars per episode to my earnings and give me an understanding of what having your name tied to dozens of episodes over seven seasons means for the producers who get most of those credits.

Some of the crew tease me about the promotion, knowing it's somewhat meaningless. A few make actively hostile comments along the lines of, Now I gotta talk to *you* when I need something? And then there are people I've known for years, including a couple of set dressers and their boss, who worked on the crime series with me, who seem genuinely happy, displaying a rare graciousness and generosity, and I am touched by it.

More substantial changes have been accumulating for a few seasons. The producers have finally pushed out a crew member who steadily interacted with the actors and who considered himself invulnerable due to his close working relationship with Jim. Apart from an edgy attitude toward production and increasingly frequent substandard performance of his non-Jim-related tasks, there has been suspicion that he has been providing drink and drugs during working hours to the cast and crew interested in such things. His removal doesn't stop the drinking and drug-taking. I end up having to have a chat with an assistant location manager we've hired about disappearances and inattention and connection to cocaine rumors, that drug in the early 2000s having become readily available and reasonably priced. It will show up at season five's wrap party, where Tana, who enjoyed it to the point of scaring herself during the drug's 1980s boom, will out of curiosity try a snort. It only ever made me frantic, so I demur.

A couple of big moves have been made down the hall. Todd Kessler has been gone awhile and a new staff writer has been added after David read and liked a sample sent his way, a script HBO later passes on and is produced by Lionsgate for AMC. It's the *Mad Men* pilot and the writer is Matthew Weiner. Immediately on showing up Matt takes an engaged interest in the people around him. He is the first writer I have more than show-related or passing conversations with. On the increasingly common distant location shoots the scripts call for, he makes time for group dinners and other off-set activities. He introduces us to the ultra-above-the-line (the "line" being, literally, the mark across a budget top-sheet that separates producers, directors, and cast from the rest of the crew) game of credit card roulette, where at the end of dinner everyone puts down a credit card and the waiter is enlisted to pick one at random, the owner of the card stuck with that night's tab. *Mad Men* will inarguably be the best of the shows produced by the writers post-*Sopranos*, though all the shows created by them benefit from lessons learned from David, including taking the format beyond a simple interweaving of plotlines by building thematic and psychological links into their scripts in the sneakily resonant way *The Sopranos* does. Years later, when Tana and I are in LA, Matt, gracious as ever, takes a break to guide us through newly constructed sets for his enormously successful show's new season, the one during which Don Draper, separated from his wife, moves into a spacious Manhattan apartment. Matt talks enthusiastically about the sunken living room as we walk across it and we act sufficiently awed and consent repeatedly when, in a deadly serious tone, he tells us, "No one is doing this. This cannot get out. You must swear to me you won't say anything to anyone."

Matt's moment of self-important self-endorsement is understandable. His series is groundbreaking, even if not in the elemental way of *The Sopranos*. And if it doesn't hit the highs of *The Sopranos* great episodes, it manages to minimize lulls and repetitions and remains throughout its run engaging and evolving. And then there is the constant praise and the inevitable inflation of self-esteem that goes with Hollywood success, inevitably warping.

We are pretty sure, though, that no one would care and nothing would be spoiled if anyone found out about a sunken living room in *Mad Men*'s lead character's bachelor digs. We are pretty sure that if we went to *People* magazine offering to reveal this architectural coup, and *People* thought enough people would care enough to buy an issue because of it and decided that, Yes, this scoop needs to get rushed to press, it would not erode anyone's enjoyment of the show.

We didn't, before our *Mad Men* set walk, sign anything, but I'll take Matt's swearing us to secrecy as an opportune time to bring up Hollywood's use of non-disclosure agreements, which in the 2000s begin to appear in start-work packets. In the case of crews, NDAs are chiefly meant to warn people away from sharing set gossip and script content with the public, protecting personal privacy and potentially valuable intellectual property from premature exposure, a valid enough concern for shows whose plot points are drawing cards for return audiences.

I have more than once walked into the writers' conference room at *The Sopranos* as an assistant pinned a piece of construction paper over the whiteboard to keep the non-writing crew from seeing outlines of future episodes. Not long after the end of *Sopranos*, studios will resort more and more often to extreme measures of script security and strictures on the sharing of information about sets, costumes, haircuts, and other visual elements that strike me as blustery and self-important. I'm confident that what is typed into the screenwriting program Final Draft or mocked up in illustrations or in scale models made of fabric and foam board is without interest to an audience. Quentin Tarantino, a fanatically secretive writer-director, in apparent anger about the appearance online of an early draft of his screenplay for *The Hateful Eight*, announced he'd turn the script into a novel rather than make the movie, eventually reversing the decision, the leak having no discernible effect on the public's interest in or the financial success of the film. I would argue that this is because only those interested in writing screenplays read screenplays. Few people outside the movie business, a few pages into the odd document a screenplay is, have any interest in continuing. And as to the necessity of keeping *The Sopranos* plot points carefully covered up, the day does come when someone in that office or passing through it takes a photo or jots down notes of what's up on the board and leaks it to the *New York Daily News*, which with typical tabloid unscrupulousness publishes what it has in its entirety, and as horrified as David, the writers, the producers, and the HBO execs may be, no one out in the world makes much of it after the initial jolt of attention passes, and the show isn't affected.

In the end, the NDAs' prime and almost exclusive function in the entertainment business becomes the silencing of witnesses to and victims of egregious behaviors of those in power, and though this may seem like a self-serving and somewhat self-righteous defense of disclosures, however slight, on offer in this account, it matches my experience and observation. I never signed NDAs in the early days and was never forced to. Ironically, now that everyone knows the evil these documents have protected and prolonged, studios seem more determined than ever to have everyone sign them.

The thirteen episodes of season five shoot endlessly. The crew works for most of 2003, good for our bank accounts and, for those in unions, our health and pension plans. Early in the year, already weeks into prep, there's a widely publicized contract dispute between Jim and HBO that delays us, and ends with a lot of money for Jim, a portion of which, in his endlessly generous way, he shares via checks written to the other principal actors on the show. Their renegotiated contracts give them nice raises but nothing like Jim's and (no doubt) David's, though Edie Falco and Lorraine Bracco deservedly do quite nicely, too.

Jim becomes increasingly giving as his fame and his apparent discomfort with it grow. He also becomes increasingly unreliable, so that in his new deal HBO reportedly adds a clause making him responsible for shoot-day costs if he misses work due to excesses of consumption, though who knows how they word it. This doesn't put an end to it. Word is HBO never charges him for a day. I am near Edie one morning outside the Soprano house when we get yet another call that Jim won't be coming in, and after relaying the news watch her shake her head and say with more than a little disgust, "Are you kidding me?"

You can't blame her. She's there a couple hours early for hair and makeup, with 5:00 AM or earlier pickups not unusual. She is always on time, always fully prepared, always amazingly and instantly in character. She is nothing but an admirable on-set presence through the entire run of the show. Jim seems in awe of and frustrated by her ready access to convincing emotion. He often gets to set not quite in character, cursing himself mid-scene, calling on the script supervisor to feed him lines. But it's worth the wait, worth making up the occasional missed day, because he more than anyone other than David makes the show what it is, his expressive features and rich readings and menacing, restrained gesturing delivering great and consistent impact. Running into him at craft service one day after he's done multiple takes of a scene he looks up with tears in his eyes, tears running down his face, and shakes his head, referring to himself in the third person when he says, "Look at him, can't cry for the camera and now he can't stop."

As down on himself as he often is, he is beloved by the cast and crew and is alone in *The Sopranos* universe in his steady generosity to those he works with. Every Friday night, week after filming week, he has mounds of sushi delivered to set, enough to allow the hundred-plus people on the shooting crew to fill plates with it. At the end of each season he gives everyone a significant gift. A few times it's gift certificates

worth hundreds of dollars. In the final season he hands out
scores of sports watches with a cenotaphic engraving on the
back.

High points for me in season five include spending time with a
couple of the one-off directors who fill gaps left by the regulars.
Peter Bogdanovich, an old friend of David's, has been playing
Lorraine Bracco's supervising shrink for a few seasons now.
Finally, David gives him an episode to direct. Bogdanovich
shoots in abbreviated takes and progressively changing camera
angles that leave little room for overseers to recut the work,
useful when battling intrusive producers or studios if you're a
feature director without final cut who wants the movie to end
up as close to your conception as possible, and less than ideal if
you're a showrunner who oversees editing and wants to maintain the well-established style of a successful show.

Along with a staccato shooting style and his standard
sartorial flourishes including sports jacket and neckerchief,
Bogdanovich provides some nice glory-day anecdotes and an
occasional glimpse into his long life in Hollywood – for example, when we overhear during a drive in the scout van his side
of a long conversation full of *mm-hmms, reallys, of courses*,
and *what did you expects* and then on hanging up says to all of
us, "Sorry, that was Nicholson."

"Jack Nicholson?" someone asks.

"The man goes on," Bogdanovich says. "And on and on
and on."

Mike Figgis, director of *Leaving Las Vegas*, solicits an
episode and, years after the regretted Lee Tamahori cameo,
David goes along. I never learn what he thinks of the result, but
the episode plays well and fits in fine with those that surround
it. During the shoot, Figgis seems as interested in practicing
blues numbers on the acoustic guitar he carts around with him
as in setting up shots, putting the guitar aside when the actors
are called. Given that I'm covering the episode and spending
hours at his side, I manage to have a few conversations with
him, bringing up films of his I've enjoyed (*Stormy Monday,
One Night Stand, Leaving Las Vegas*), remembering only an
interstitial comment he makes when talking about going on
distant location with cast and crew for his movie *Cold Creek
Manor*: "This is early on, when everyone is still sorting out
who they're going to be sleeping with."

I nod like I know what he's talking about.

Another one-off director who nabs an episode of *The
Sopranos* is Rodrigo García, a large, thoughtful man who has
directed a few lovely, closely observed films and a batch of TV
episodes, some for HBO. He also happens to be Gabriel García
Márquez's son, an item barely mentioned in the lead-up to
his arrival and not discussed over the course of his uneventful

time on the show. For lit majors in the late 1970s in the United States, García Márquez was a world-building figure, the most prominent name in the most prominent literary movement of recent decades, magical realism, and being in the presence of his son means something to me, though I'm not sure I ever express it or try to, because what can you say to the child of someone like that that they haven't heard endlessly? Nevertheless, I watch him closely for an aura or sign of special dispensation, and discern nothing. He's kind and mild and intelligent. He's not arrogant or strident, unlike some episodic directors who seem determined to impress upon the seasoned and somewhat cynical crew their observational acumen and feature-film-worthy ability. He does a decent job and disappears, leaving a pleasant impression on everyone.

My father in his high school baseball uniform, circa 1946.

Jim Gandolfini with New Jersey state troopers outside Howard Johnson's, Asbury Park, NJ, circa 1999. (photo: Regina Heyman)

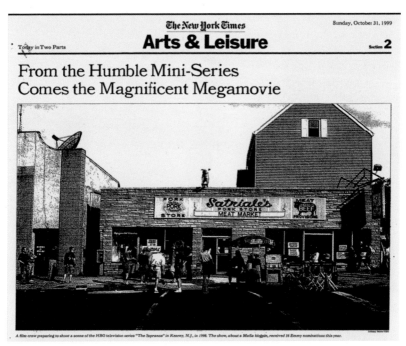

An early hagiographic article by Vincent Canby on the front page of *The New York Times* "Arts & Leisure" section on Sunday, Oct. 31, 1999.

TLS November 15 2002

FICTION

Small shifts in loving

MARK KAMINE

Sam Shepard

GREAT DREAM OF HEAVEN
142pp. Secker and Warburg. Paperback, £10.
0 436 20594 7

Great Dream of Heaven is the second collection of short stories by the playwright-actor Sam Shepard. It joins *Cruising Paradise* (1996), *Hawk Moon* and *Motel Chronicles* (poems, prose poems, autobiographical sketches, short stories) and the *Rolling Thunder Log Book*, about the 1975 Bob Dylan tour. The three early books are chiefly of interest as adjuncts to Shepard's renowned plays and tabloid-ready life (co-star of *Days of Heaven* and *The Right Stuff*, consort of Patti Smith and Jessica Lange, friend of Bob Dylan). *Cruising Paradise*, however, contains a number of pieces that stand on their own. There are tales of misspent youth set in the 1950s and 60s, and "Dust", a classic story about a driven loner in the contemporary American West that turns the expected macho stance on its head. The book is filled out with sketches and playlets and a series of sharp, well-told tales of Hollywood, the autobiographical allure of which perhaps dilutes the purer pleasures of the more hermetic stories.

The new collection *Great Dreams of Heaven* leans less on Shepard's personal myth, allowing the stories to play the starring roles. The first, "The Remedy Man", is narrated by the teenage son of a hardscrabble horse farmer who has called in a local horse-breaker named E. V. to deal with a too-wild gelding. The straightforward action – how E. V. goes about settling the horse down – serves as fulcrum for the world-changing shift in the son's perspective.

Shepard is adept at pitch-perfect dialogue rich in emotional undercurrents. The pleasant surprise in his prose is his easy way with narrative voice, as he lays out the boy's hidden heart after E. V. chooses him instead of his father to assist with the horse-breaking: "He turned to me and as soon as his light eyes fixed on me it was as though a warm hand landed softly on my chest. There was a kindness there that surprised me how much I yearned toward it."

Even when the plots of a few of the stories take predictable turns – "Coalinga 1/2 Way" about a man running from one woman to the next, and "Blinking Eye" about a pair of squabbling sisters – the language has a forceful plainness, rooted in short hard Anglo-Saxon sounds and rhythms, that propels the narrative: "He sees himself from a distance now, as though looking down from a great height, like the hawk's point of view; a tiny man in vast space, clutching a chunk of black plastic"; "she speaks out loud while her bright eyes scan the enormous white sea of salt."

There are a number of short stories in different voices – a trinket salesman, an all-night gas station attendant – that have nifty twists at the end. Occasionally these are of a Gothic nature, as when the attendant's fear of losing her job turns into carefully imagined fear of physical violence. In "Convulsion", a two-page lover's plea from a man waiting for a train, Shepard folds the event into itself in a fashion reminiscent of Julio Cortázar.

But it is in the more sustained narratives that the author reaches full stride. "Concepción", another tale of a rift between father and son, pits a silent, superstitious air force pilot against his over-curious child. On the way home from church, the family stops at a Gypsy's house, mother and son waiting in the car while the father goes inside. By the time he reappears, the son has torn the collar of his choir robe and the mother has made him promise to keep it secret so that his father doesn't get angry. The family's surface rigidity – broken for a moment when the collar rips, and later when the boy spies on his father completing his Gypsy rites – is beautifully traced in small details: the car-bound mother watching the father return to the car, "smoothed her skirt down and placed her purse back in her lap as though she hadn't moved an inch the whole time he'd been gone".

Equally expert in execution is the title story, "Great Dream of Heaven", about the sudden rivalry of two old men for a waitress's affection. Shepard's effortless shifts in perspective between the men mirror the power struggle between them. And in "An Unfair Question", perhaps the finest story here, the off-key humour of its frustrated tough-guy narrator sent out to "go hunt down more basil" for a party of women leads to the kind of chillingly hysterical finale Shepard has shown mastery of in the theatre. Such stories make one hope he finds time between acting gigs for more of the same.

Scrapbook clipping of my first article for the *Times Literary Supplement*, 2002.

Silvercup, a former bakery in Long Island City, which housed *The Sopranos* offices and stages, 2003. (photo: Mike King)

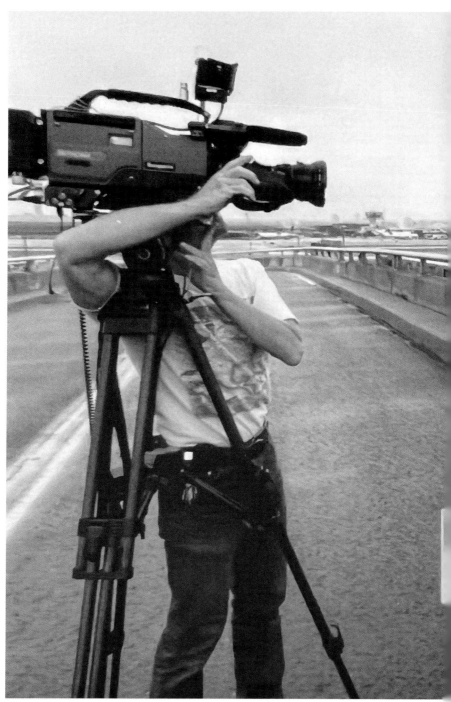

My interview for "Turnpike," a 2005 segment of the PBS show *State of the Arts* narrated by Paul Sorvino and including the title sequence of *The Sopranos*.

Edie Falco with a fan of the show at the wrap party for season five, December 2003. (photo: Sandra Vannucchi)

Jim filming the monastery scene for season six's alternative life sequence at David Chase's former house in Los Angeles, 2006.

Lauren Bacall suffering through a photo with me after we shot her exterior scenes outside the Beverly Hilton Hotel, 2006. My wife said it's the biggest smile she's ever seen on my face.

Tim Van Patten, David Chase, co-writers, and crew during the Paris scout, 2006.

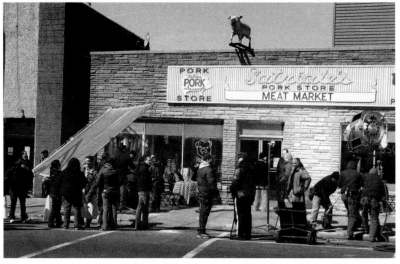

The crew setting up a shot in front of the post-pilot Pork Store, 2007. (Flickr photo service)

David's final crew wrap gift, a *Sopranos* belt buckle by silversmith Pat Areias, circa 2007.

A paparazzo took this shot of Christian Bale walking past the grip truck, and me, during filming of *The Fighter*. I am on my phone, as usual, 2009.

13

Between Seasons: An Enemy of Art

The lingering post and rest periods after shooting seasons four and five mean six months off from the show in 2002 and next to no work in 2004. The freelance life almost, but never quite, accustoms you to gaps between jobs, so a season of *The Sopranos* sort where shooting thirteen episodes takes about as long as the twenty-two or twenty-three episodes of a normal network season while providing a prestigious association is hard to argue with, however you feel about the long hours or the position you hold. HBO's willingness to accommodate the downtime desires of their principal payees, meaning months between seasons and inconsistent air dates, is one more hurdle in the path of steady paychecks, which kids, mortgages, and vacations require. At some point a month or two into unemployment there will be uncomfortable moments at home. It's been years since Tana and I went into credit card debt, and we haven't had to dip into the line of credit we got as soon as our debt was erased, feeling we needed a cushion in case of a writers' strike or a New York production downturn, but like everyone with bills to pay and not much in reserve, I need to get a job. I call around and email people I've worked for in the past, a soon-exhausted selection. After that, I hunker down and hope my name will pop up or get passed along when some LA producer with an East Coast–bound job starts asking around. Tana understands but, as the savings account dwindles, asks if I don't want to get back on the phone. I know she doesn't get how I can go weeks without wanting to check in with the people I've already called or to try to dig up new names. The idea that it might cause me some embarrassment doesn't make it as an excuse when it's clear we need to get back in the black. Voices might occasionally be raised.

In 2002 I work the first half of the year on season four and, after it ends, reluctantly accept some scouting days on a movie, for me as painful a way to earn money as ever. Next I get a call from Graham telling me Barry Sonnenfeld will be back in town with a big job that will go deep into 2003. Even though *The Sopranos* is due to start up sometime after the New Year, I can't afford to wait three months for it and am more than willing to leave the show behind entirely. I still harbor resentment about the couple of former location managers brought in to production manage above me, a not fully rational reaction as they both had experience in that position that I didn't, and in addition I can still tell myself that features are more prestigious, even if newspapers and magazines are proclaiming a revolution afoot and dubbing the 2000s the golden age of television, primarily due to *The Sopranos*. Accolades accorded writers and actors don't translate to the ground level where most of us make our living. We get roughly a 3 percent increase a year and the show's success has no impact on our bottom lines. Features still attract the best New York crews, though *The Sopranos* does, once its stature is established, lure top people – our new key grip, for example, well into a career full of New York classics including my first mainstream feature *Quiz Show* along with *Goodfellas*, *When Harry Met Sally*, and, he tells me with some amusement, both the original and the remake of *Gloria*. Even as TV evolves, many production people scoff at the work, and in job interviews I go to over these years to fill between-season months I am told more than once that I am not the first choice because I lack the feature experience of the top New York people. It's enough to keep me wide open to jumping onto a big-budget feature even if I won't be done in time for whenever the next season starts.

Sonnenfeld's new project is based on kids' books called *A Series of Unfortunate Events*, written by Daniel Handler under the pen name Lemony Snicket. The script Graham sends me maintains its sources' sentimental and sanitized darkness, but no one is asking my opinion and they're paying my rate. I hire Gina and we start scouting, meeting most nights back at a sparsely staffed production office downtown. We're four or more months away from filming, a relatively leisurely prep period. We go over location photos with Barry, Graham, Neri, and the production designer, Rick Heinrichs, a former art director under Barry's prior designer, Bo, who is busy pursuing a directing career, having picked up episodic gigs on Barry's series *The Tick* and coming close to getting a feature greenlit. He will eventually turn the classic kids' book *The Cat in the Hat* into a healthily budgeted flop, after which he will subside back into production design, commenting the next time I see him, sense of humor extant, "I'm a waiter again." Critics will eventually come back around to that sole feature, calling it ahead of its time and maybe even a visual master-piece. Rick Heinrichs meanwhile takes over Bo's blockbuster clientele including Barry and Tim Burton, for whose ravish-ingly pointless *Sleepy Hollow* he will pick up an Academy Award, an achievement Bo hasn't managed.

I'm getting a better understanding of what production design-ers do. From the start, I'd driven them around looking at locations they liked while making clear to them my under-standing of their importance to the production, an unceasing task that remains critical to each job I move into, the people toward whom such sycophancy is directed altering as I rise in the ranks. Rick doesn't seem to need much boosting. He is often silent and always serious as he sits at his drafting table or spends hours in the office hovering over a scale model of the *Unfortunate* set he has envisioned and has had constructed in miniature on a plywood base, the model complete with roads, rivers, houses, trees, cars, and the miniature people found in model train kits. He orders a lipstick lens attachment for his videocam and using this articulating extension shoots a series of angles of the model, sometimes using swooping crane-like movements of his arm. Standing nearby and seeing the image in the onboard monitor, I suddenly get what it means to think not only about architectural detail or degree of finish but also about how something will appear on screen.

If Barry has interest in any of this I'm not there to witness it. He sits in his big office, usually with Graham on the couch along the back wall and a couple of us in the chairs between them, Barry telling stories, talking shit, and sometimes getting around to the project we're working on. I walk away from one of these sessions feeling a bit of my own emergent visual acuity when Barry, in paging through our latest stack of location pictures, pauses over shots of a Long Island beach whose stretch of sand is broken up with large boulders, one of which I stood half behind to shoot a partially rock-blocked frame, and comments, "You took this? It's a nice shot. I like this."

My friend Eli stops by the office. He's a writer recently back from Italy, having won the Rome Prize in 1998 for his first novel. After his year at the American Academy, he moved into an apartment in Trastevere and a span of expatriate life. He's a well-spoken addition to any room and is looking forward to this visit, as I have talked Barry up to him as the kind of outsized character I know he will enjoy. Barry, I'm pretty certain, will find Eli worth hearing from, too. As we settle into chairs, Barry begins the inquisition he likes to inflict on newcomers. At some point in answering him, talking possibly about the ways in which Rome differs from New York, Eli uses the word *somnolent*, not a particularly abstruse one but all that Barry needs.

"Somnolent," he says in disbelief. "Somnolent. Isn't that a country in Africa?"

At a bar later, Eli and I talk over the patently anti-intellectual tenor of Barry's comically cushioned aggressions, riffing our way to a hypothesis about the regular-gal-and-guy veneer with which Hollywood coats its insular and envied existence, where everyone is down-to-earth, wears T-shirts almost everywhere, and just wants to be left alone, while at the same time smoothly accepting the special privileges provided. Eli also acknowledges that novelists fresh from Rome with multisyllabic words at the tips of their tongues can only pray for a shot at even a midsized payout for movie rights, Hollywood hitmakers understanding that the possibility of sharing a piece of the pie will buy a lot of tolerance from whomever they deign to bring into the room.

Barry gets fired for a reason I'm not privy to beyond a rumor about the incompatibility of his vision with a publisher exercising tight control over a prized property. He's also at this moment more vulnerable than he had been, having come off two large flops (*Big Trouble* and *Wild Wild West*) after a string of successes in the 1990s, when he directed two *Addams Family* movies, *Get Shorty*, and the two *Men in Blacks*. Before this happens, though, I am asked to attend a meeting at producer Scott Rudin's midtown office, which I look forward to, having heard the stories about his tossing of books, phones, and anything else he can get his hands on at a bevy of assistants always disappointing him and whom he periodically fires, at which point they all scurry out the door and across the street to the nearby bar where they wait for the top assistant to get the call asking where everyone is and to get back to work already.

The meeting we have isn't fiery or abusive, but Rudin and Barry spar steadily. There is a moment when in discussing locations Rudin turns to me and asks about the theater some scenes are set at, theaters being a major part of his producing life, and I tell him Barry's favorite is a West Village one located at the elbow of a short, scenic street. Rudin looks at me with thorough meanness and makes me swear that it is locked in and that he won't have to hear about it falling through, to which I respond — a location truth — that until we have prep and shoot dates and a signed contract, I certainly can't guarantee anything. He says something like, "Okay listen, I'm telling you right now, this theater is the perfect place for these scenes and it had better work out." To which I have no response. They move on to casting, and Rudin brings up James Gandolfini as perfect for a big role.

"Isn't he committed to *The Sopranos?*" Graham says.

"I hear he's leaving the show," Rudin says.

"Mark?" Graham says to me.

"He's coming back," I say.

"Not likely," Rudin says.

"Scott, don't you think he might know better than you?" Graham says.

I get a second stern look from Rudin.

"I mean, he's coming back," I say.

"I don't think so," Rudin says.

"You just can't be wrong, can you, Scott?" Barry says, laughing.

He is wrong, though maybe he knew something, because this will be the season that requires an extended negotiation with Gandolfini's people.

—

The acclaim around *The Sopranos* results, for me, in years of calls for jobs I don't want, often getting asked to work as a scout, which at a certain point I refuse to do, or as a location manager, which I no longer want to do but will go along with if the state of our bank account dictates it. The calls are always for projects with *Sopranos*-like settings or moods. One of these comes from a producer who tells me his director, Wayne Kramer, wants to hire *The Sopranos* location manager for his action-fueled follow-up to *The Cooler*, a critical success that gave a decent return on its tiny budget. I heard good things about that movie (I'll enjoy it when I eventually see it). I like the sound of the project. And we could use the cash. I sign on.

The designer needs choices for all the scripted locations but already knows that due to budget constraints the movie will mostly be shot somewhere cheaper. The film biz is not exempt from the increasing outsourcing of jobs as America becomes too expensive to satisfy the globally retooled bottom lines of businesses, and since ours is essentially an industrial pursuit, both labor-intensive and dependent on a variety of technical equipment and physical goods to create an actual if not tactilely graspable product (flickering light, digital data), the studios have for years been chasing savings. This causes an outcry among labor unions, who hire lobbyists to push states to adopt film tax credits that other countries, most proximately Canada, have pioneered. These boil down to 20 or so percent of government givebacks on money spent while on location, justified by job creation, hotel bookings, restaurant reservations, and purchases of movie-biz staples such as lumber, clothing, and furniture. A dozen or more states are coaxed into initiating the credits, and in certain places they stick. All kinds of statistics are found to support the governmental outlay, but there's plenty of evidence that the hit to taxpayers is never fully recouped. Not that this negates the good it does or makes the movie business uniquely cozened. Farms and factories get more money. And movies do have glamour and popular appeal absent from the tractor and tool-and-die machine. Even so, productions more and more often end up overseas, as even hefty credits can't compete with European, Asian, or African crew and material costs.

Cheap labor and exchange rates notwithstanding, the expectation is a certain portion of *Running Scared* will need to be filmed in and around New York, the days dependent more on what the budget can bear than on how much of Prague (where eventually the movie lands) can pass for New Jersey. Kramer wants a couple weeks, the financier finally crushing this down to four days. I field a small team of scouts, eventually meeting up with Toby, the production designer, to tour an assortment of locations. He takes measurements and photos of places he sees as suitable models for the Prague build. We settle on a few streets in downtown Newark and its suburban-looking outer edges as irreplicable in Eastern Europe and we pick a day's worth of locations in Brooklyn for I forget what part of the story.

Feeling secure in the job due to my *Sopranos*-stamped expertise, I angle early on for increased responsibilities and an elevated title, putting mild pressure on Jeff, the local line producer hired soon after the one who originally hired me is fired. He's a kind of low-budget specialist, looped in with the scrappier Hollywood studios who make smaller, sometimes arty, sometimes exploitative films. The people behind these entities are often unscrupulous entrepreneurs who made their money by being born or through cunning and connivance and who are by nature attracted to stars, parties, and any business lacking heavy governmental oversight. In later years I'll wonder at Jeff's knack for falling in with this breed of, essentially, con artists. As an example of the kinds of shady tactics employed, Jeff tells me how his most recent boss moved money into his production's account to show union reps an ability to meet payroll and, having satisfied them, swiftly moved the money into another movie's account to prove the same thing there, Jeff learning about what happened when his show's paychecks were delayed and he checked the bank account. The low-budget background has kept Jeff from joining the DGA, and the necessity on the Kramer project of staffing the production manager position is my wedge into an elevated role once the scouting period moves into the final stages of prep, allowing me to argue that I will save him money by covering DGA production and location managing positions. He goes for it. I give Gina a raise for the increased burden she'll bear. Jeff is soon coaching me through cost-cutting strategies and consulting with me on his producorial problems.

Running Scared tracks a man who has taken a bullet to the gut, slowly dying as he drives around New York and New Jersey avoiding mobsters and cops. It has a good, gritty look and some cool action to go with its combustive concept. Its leads, Paul Walker and Vera Farmiga, are effective. Walker turns out to be friendly and mellow, agreeing to get on the phone with my then thirteen-year-old son, who has become a surfing fanatic. They talk waves for a while and then Walker offers to put him in touch with a board shaper he likes, to whom we will eventually fork over five hundred bucks for a short board we get Jack as gift.

Months before the shoot, the team comes in to scout. Kramer and his DP have a lot of what I'm getting used to in youngish LA creative types, a fair amount of intelligence and forceful personalities, a belief in their vision, a determination to disregard or roll over any suggestion of monetary constraint, an apparent indifference to anything intellectual or art-related unless it has to do with or can be applied to the making of movies. They dress in the then unavoidable 7 For All Mankind jeans and black T-shirts. Kramer is a fit, intense, humorless man of South African descent. He's a forthright person enamored of his nocturnal existence, seeing his wife and young child (children?) for a few hours in the afternoon before cruising into another movie-watching, screenplay-composing overnight. He seems to be selling scripts as quickly as he can format his fervid concepts into Final Draft, but he wants to direct for a living and the success of his last movie makes him and the rest of us believe he will do just that. His DP is perfectly in sync with his attitude and vision.

Jeff and I march around behind Kramer and the DP on the scout before they jet off to Prague, amazed at the ambitious expansiveness of their plans. The DP requests two lighting barges and a string of condors carrying large lighting instruments spread out along both banks of the river on whose Newark-side bank we're thinking of shooting a night scene. At other locations he asks for Technocranes, a helicopter, and a Russian arm (a speedy SUV equipped with a top-mounted telescoping arm to carry the camera high or low alongside fast-moving picture cars). Jeff comes up to me again and again to inform me, "None of this is happening," or, "They're out of their fucking minds." Which is about the way it ends up. We'll have some big lights and a condor or two a day, but there will be no barges, no helicopters, and no Russian arm.

Not that the few days we shoot aren't ambitious. We put a small crane on a camera car and drive at reasonable speed around the neighborhoods of downtown Newark in front of, behind, and alongside Paul Kramer piloting the show's vintage Mustang. One night we divert traffic from and light up a Passaic River bridge in Kearny, that *Sopranos* stronghold, where storywise the hero runs up against a police blockade and must make a skidding, swooping turn and find another way home. We light the side of a house on fire with a little more gusto than planned, melting aluminum siding and giving one of our effects men second-degree burns that he shrugs off, refusing the ride to the hospital in the ambulance that comes for him, deciding after the EMTs examine him to finish the night's work and go to a doctor the next day. On that night, the final one of the film at the exterior of the house whose many interior scenes have already been filmed on a stage in Prague, the endless bickering between director and studio-backed producer reaches a rare level of malevolence. As dawn adds detail and color to the Newark street we're set up on, Andrew, the producer, announces he is shutting down the shoot. Kramer, not far off, tells his AD to keep the crew working.

"It's not happening, Wayne," Andrew says.

"I need another shot," Kramer says.

"No," Andrew says, and turns to me. "Spread the word."

I look at the AD, who hasn't said anything.

Kramer stomps up to Andrew.

"You are not doing this again," he says. "I will call your boss."

"I'll dial him for you," Andrew says, phone out.

Understanding he is indeed done, Kramer launches into a more frontal attack. Andrew is not a filmmaker. He doesn't understand movies. He is an enemy of art.

Andrew's response is to tell the AD to call wrap right now over channel one or to hand him his walkie so he can do it, and, after a moment of hesitation, the AD makes the call. We are wrapped.

As we say goodbye Andrew tells me that if I want to keep doing this job he thinks it will go well for me, that I am good at it, and leaves. I don't know what to think. I don't want to be an enemy of art. But I do like the bigger paychecks I know I will get when I fully move up.

Like all film fans, I love hearing old-Hollywood stories of directors traducing the crass commercial concerns of monstrous studio moguls and turning genre dross meant only to drum up decent box office into artful studies of human nature in appropriately lit and composed cinematic space. But now that I am looking to put myself in a position right in the middle of creative and financial forces, I find I'm surprisingly sympathetic to the studio side of things. Anything, I tell myself, that requires putting hundreds of people on payroll and spending fortunes on equipment and materials necessarily means that whatever funding entity is behind a project has a right to curb overruns. I like to believe that it is possible to be in some ultimate sense on the side of the filmmaker, making as much of what they want to happen as I can, while still acting as a check on extravagance.

Running Scared won't, on its release, make much money or attract much attention, but for me it's a significant step up the production ladder, and I end up proud to have been a part of it.

14

My *Sopranos* Years, Part Five

David hasn't directed an episode since the pilot so the team hasn't spent time scouting with him for years. He rode in the bus with us for the tech scout of the first (post-pilot) episode of season one. He'll scout again when he directs the final episode. In between, the only scout I remember him going on is during early prep of a late season when the writers are mulling a plotline involving a large construction project on the Newark waterfront. I'm called on to arrange a boat ride along the Passaic River. I have contacts at a yacht club on the Newark Bay we've scouted in the past and track down a boat without too much draft, a necessity in navigating the sludge-filled river.

Early one morning, I meet David and Ilene at a marina on the southeastern edge of Newark and climb aboard a long red-hulled boat, pointlessly powerful and flashy, and at David's request the friendly and seemingly expert captain jets us out into the ghoulishly scenic center of Newark Bay, where we look across the slate-gray water at the grand prospect of land-fill, scrub, industry, and city skyline until the boat's engine vacuums up a large piece of plastic, begins to smoke, and stalls out, focusing our attention more narrowly. I envision the boat catching fire and us needing to jump. I'm a good swimmer and it's not dead winter so figure that the water temperature won't kill me if I stay calm, but what about David and Ilene? I look at them, and it occurs to me that I will be responsible for arranging the death by fire or drowning of TV's greatest creative force and his right-hand woman. I hear David mutter the word *ignominious* in what I conjecture is his own imagined account of his death. The captain has by this time opened the engine compartment and blasted the onboard fire extinguisher's contents into it. We float along as via cell phone the man wrangles a tow in from a friend who keeps a small cabin cruiser at the marina. I make a deal with this man to take over the scout, and after pulling the stalled craft in, that is what he does, motoring up the Passaic River past junkyards, factories, and warehouses to the somewhat impressive wall of downtown Newark skyscrapers and the city's central train station, bending north with the river, Route 21 on one side and a string of service stations, small parks, and strip malls on the other. We eventually dock as planned at the Kearny Boathouse, a wooden dock jutting out of a muddy bank near a squat cement building housing racing shells where we have already filmed the memorable scene where Christopher undergoes a false execution engineered by Uncle Junior. In the end, the waterfront barely figures in the coming season, but we do spot one or two interesting locations to follow up on.

A successful TV showrunner has final say over all details — story, script, cast, costumes, props and sets, every sound and music cue, the look of title cards, the feel of the publicity campaigns, and the thousand other elements that go into each hour of each episode and much of what takes place to promote and otherwise monetize the product. There are those meetings before shooting starts, some described earlier, during which the showrunner and writers sign off on wardrobe, props, and locations. There are casting sessions with the director. There is also, at the end of each prep period, an hourslong production meeting to go through the script page by page to finalize what to have ready when — how many picture cars will be parked outside the pork store when we shoot there, how big the crowd will be at the Bada Bing, what's being served for dinner at the Soprano house. Most crucially there's a tone meeting with David and the writers along with the episode's director, director of photography, assistant director, and producers, an LA-based post producer and editor on the other end of a speakerphone, during which the director talks everyone through the plan of attack, pitching performance parameters and thematic stresses. I see as I begin to attend these meetings how David will listen closely and step in if the director fails to correctly discern the subtext of a scene or hasn't highlighted clues important to later episodes that need to be noticed by the camera.

Most prep meetings are uneventful. Location-wise, David occasionally, after studying a folder, rejects a place the group – director, designer, episode writer – has picked. Director or designer might speak up if it's a prized choice, but David is rarely persuaded. We leave the meeting and I tell the scouts to start scrambling for alternatives, then we get back in the van to see in person whatever worthwhile comes in. We may still be looking the day before the episode begins shooting or in dire circumstance once it's begun, getting up a few hours early to hit a promising spot before call time or going out at lunch to check one near where we're shooting. If we've had no luck, we bring the originally rejected folder back, sometimes with photos snapped from what we hope are better angles. David makes a face of resignation and caves or stays firm and we keep searching.

Having edged into the next level of the production ranks, I now sit in on all prep meetings for episodes I'm covering, including that tone meeting, the most interesting one of all as it gets to broader issues involving thematic concepts and character arcs. I remember in season six one director's failure to perform passably, pushing David beyond standard skepticism into open scorn. He is a first-timer renowned for the high percentage of pilots he has directed that have become successful series. His agents have reached out repeatedly to HBO and Ilene to get him a slot on *The Sopranos*. He has a breezy, confident manner that leads him without hiccups through the scouting, shot-listing, and departmental meetings, strolling into the tone meeting apparently expecting more of the same. His dark hair and round face remind me of my mother's second husband, Fred Paul, a similarly glib personality with a trove of disturbance roiling beneath a calm demeanor. This top TV director's ambition seems to be all about connecting his name to *The Sopranos* high-prestige brand, as he doesn't seem particularly in tune with or suited to the show. He turns out to be incapable of picking up the thrust or meaning of much of anything in the script, David soon impatiently pointing out lines to be underscored on camera, themes to be brought forth, and dismissing dreams of graceful tracking and crane shots as wasted time and not worth hearing about. I watch this cool character begin to sweat as David stops making eye contact, looking down at the script pages and nailing down again and again the crux of scene after scene. A flashy filmic style means nothing in that office. It's all about capturing in camera what's on the page.

Seams show during a few writers'-room meetings in late seasons. At one gathering David asks about the medical science behind a scene, looking at the married couple whose script is being prepped. The woman expresses confidence that what's there is fairly accurate, to which David replies, "No one is expecting you to take the time to do the actual research." There's back-and-forth, and then David shifts from sarcasm to bluntness, using the word *lazy*, outright. Which causes the man to look fixedly into space, while the woman makes faint protest, appearing to have physically absorbed a blow, slouching low in her chair and remaining silent as the meeting proceeds.

These two have written many fine episodes and shared credits with David on others. They have deep history with him. Nevertheless, they will be gone after the first part of the final season. It may be David's impatience with flagging performance or a sense that they are more interested in deals they have in the works in expectation of the end of the job. And he may be feeling pressure about bringing the series to a satisfactory close and intolerant of any lack of focus.

I have witnessed demotions, firings, and fast exits frequently enough in the biz, my response often empathetic once things move beyond that initial enticing spurt of back-office gossip. I have been myself more than once in the hot seat and have been fired twice, but with these writers my empathy is next to nonexistent. I've never heard either of them thank the crew for their skill or the long hours worked. David is a counterexample in that he periodically voices kind and believably heartfelt praise, often as he picks up trophies at awards ceremonies or speaks the introductions to the couple of episodes previewed at the increasingly enormous premieres that HBO underwrites as each season's air date approaches. He also finds time for rounds of individual praise, in my case muttering to me or at least in my direction during a discussion of locations, "You're an artist," the word *artist* surprising and memorable. And the woman, who seems to be the guiding hand in this writing duo, is flatly unsupportive of me in my only encounter with her away from her husband or the group, a favor to me in the long run, but nothing about the couple minutes or so of that private conversation endears her to me. It occurs because I succumb to the always dangerous temptation of attempting a screenplay.

Screenwriting is its own form of writing, very different from book reviewing and fiction. Reading scripts isn't sufficient training. But being in the business and having a writing sideline sometimes makes me wonder how I'd do, and the long *Sopranos* run with lengthy downtimes between seasons lures me in. As I've always admired Mike R's visual acuity and the sharp dialogue in his short films and the couple of feature scripts of his I've seen, and knowing he's at this point no happier than me in the production game, I ask if he wants to write something together.

"What do you have in mind?" he asks.

"A *Sopranos* spec script," I say.

"Really?"

"Might as well," I say. "We know where this season ends, and who knows when they'll come back to shoot the next one."

This is during the second half of 2004. My records show some income in the summer and none in the fourth quarter, a rare lull in my couple of decades of DGA employment. It means I have time to spare. I also have thoughts about the direction the show is headed. In addition, due to my *Sopranos* connection, the *TLS* and *New York Times* have had me review some crime books, giving me a store of real-life mobster anecdotes. Mike and I draw up an outline, parcel out scenes, and over a month and change get through a draft of a script we pass between us for another month, tinkering and fixing until we feel it's worth showing.

I call Ilene to see if David will read it.

He won't, Ilene tells me. And informs me who the gate-keeper is.

Spec scripts when considered at all go to the writing couple and are typically handled by the woman. Good gatekeeper, I think. Forbidding, protective, not given to befriending those below her station. It certainly makes me think twice. But

I like the script. I like especially what Mike has done with Paulie Walnuts, turning his standard salty dialogue in the direction of the Arab characters we've written in to introduce an al-Qaeda-related story line.

I drop the script at the writers' office, where the surviving three writing units (the couple, Terry, Matt) have been joined by another couple from David's long stretches in the episodic trenches. I don't hear anything until I'm back to begin prep on season six. The gatekeeper spots me on the production side of the building and walks up, asking if I have a minute. I remember the conversation happening in a doorway at one end of the bullpen. It is early in prep and only a few of us have started work, so no one is nearby.

"You know you can't just write a script and be a screenwriter," is roughly how she starts things off. "You pay your dues first."

I don't respond.

"People work their way up. It takes years."

Still nothing for me to say.

She changes gears.

"Some of these things . . . We have similar situations this season, we treat the same subjects sometimes, you should know that. We're well into blocking out the season. It has nothing to do with your script."

"I'm not going to sue anyone if that's what you think," I say.

She seems taken aback by this, or in any case unsure where to go next. I don't think she says much more. I recall, when she walks away, watching her with mixed emotions, humiliation and a touch of self-loathing for having even tried, pride that at least I'd responded to her dismissal with one of my own.

The cigarette scam we sketched out, a version of which was in any case previously used in *Goodfellas*, is in the show and

is carried out by the character we attached to it. The al-Qaeda
stuff, when it appears, is radically different from our version.

The behind-the-scenes goings-on at long-running shows can
come to resemble families, mostly in the worst ways. Neurotic
patterns of behavior enacted over and again. Battle lines drawn
and held. Favorites played and fallback positions clung to.
There's the producer with newly minted tics and discomfit-
ing garrulousness. Another producer, mid-divorce, spends
endless hours locked in an office with stacks of papers, his sour
expression broken by frequent grimaces. An always volatile
personality tamped down by Edie's demand that she never see
him on set again, he still manages regular outbursts when she's
not around and at one point, when I am in his office for some
production-related reason, manages a rapid and astonishing
rant about the residual money I've stolen from him by sharing
a handful of UPM credits that would've instead gone to him.

At a stop on a location scout an argument breaks out
between our production manager and production designer,
no doubt budget-related. All that those of us scouting that day
hear, the two of them having stomped away from the van, is
raised voices and the startlingly furious tone of the designer,
more given to long soliloquies about opera and architecture,
and then the weeping of the production manager, an endear-
ing turn in my perception of this man. Later that day or the
next, Tim, the director of the episode, tells us about the conversation he's had with David while side by side at urinals, David
asking if it's true about tears being shed during the scout, and
when Tim confirms it, David commenting, "There's no crying
in episodic."

I don't remember much of what goes on during the time
it takes to film the two-part final season beyond a feeling of

muted dismay about where I'm stuck. On the other hand I still carry lovely, wistful memories of three distant location units Ilene assigns me to.

All involve two trips, one for scouting, one for a brief bout of final prep that slides steeply into whatever shoot days are involved. In all cases local scouts are sent out, after which our core scouting troupe shows up for an in-person tour. Multiple episodes in season six have LA segments, most of the material for which will be filmed in a block, the first fragment for an early episode when Tony, having been shot and hospitalized, enters a dream-life as an alternate personality, to me one of the rare lengthy dream sequences in film or TV that manages to sustain interest, Jim embodying with flinching perfection the meek and befuddled personality his dream-life transports him to, the rippling reflections of Tony Soprano effectively subdued.

At David's suggestion, we shoot the Buddhist monastery that Tony's alter ego visits at his old LA house. Its austere and symmetrical lines have an appropriately Eastern feel. The day we're there, in the hills above Santa Monica, I'm walking down the street on which the trucks and campers are parked when a PA runs up to me and tells me Jim has an issue and has told an AD he will only talk to me about it. I find Jim and answer his question or deal with his request feeling, frankly, flattered, and realize that my brief and insubstantial inter-actions and frequent presence on the set, particularly in the years since I've become a partial production manager, have brought me into a kind of relationship with him and the other actors that had not been part of my working life before.

Most of our LA work covers scenes from the episode called "Luxury Lounge," its principal plotline involving one more attempt by Christopher Moltisanti to turn his mob life into a movie career. We film for a few days and stay for the duration at the newly opened and thus briefly trendy Viceroy Hotel on Ocean Avenue in Santa Monica (Owen Wilson and entourage make an appearance in the lobby bar while we're there). The hotel's hallways, elevators, and other interior spaces are by design so underlit that they have me taking small steps, one hand held out to avoid crashing into walls. One sequence shows Christopher doing drugs and spending time with a call girl in his hotel room. Another takes place at the cabana-ringed pool, a fitting film-biz setting for the movie-star meet-and-greets episode author Matt Weiner has worked into the script. The show's standing secures a couple of iconic guest stars, Ben Kingsley and Lauren Bacall, showing up poolside well prepared and very much themselves, Kingsley's air grand and his posture impeccably upright, his assistant telling us to call him Sir Ben and generally to show regard and respect, Bacall somewhat hobbled physically but out front about everything, including the gaffers tape she collects, her eye on a few of the rolls she sees on set as the crew has some colors she doesn't yet have at home. We have been told to expect such requests from her, specifically that she likes this kind of tape and will want to take some away at the end of the day. And I get it. It's a great item, one of those film-set specialties that should be available everywhere, easy to tear crosswise and in strips, with an ideally strong stickiness that, when the time comes, lifts off in a piece and leaves no goo behind.

Bacall also appears in a night scene at the Beverly Hilton filmed in and around a limousine. It's one of those chilly Southern California evenings, a temperature – low fifties? – not even worth noting in New York but that has everyone in layers in LA. During downtime I knock on the limo door where Bacall waits alone between setups.

"What?" I hear her say from inside.

I open the door.

"While we're waiting for the next setup I'd love to ask you some questions," I say.

"Sure," she says. "Get in and shut the fucking door. It's freezing."

I sit down next to her, close the door.

"So what is it?" she says.

"This has nothing to do with movies," I say.

She looks at me.

"You knew Hemingway?"

She sits back. "Ernest Hemingway, yes," she says. "Yes, I did. I met him in Spain with Slim Hawks. We were traveling together. He was pretentious as hell. Going on about the wine he was serving. Showing off. A pretentious man. I met him other times. In New York, and somewhere else."

"I love that you describe him as pretentious," I say. "It's the last thing he would've wanted."

"Well, he was."

"That's great," I say.

She seems to think about it.

"But I'll tell you one thing," she says. "This was before I met him. We were in our living room. I was sitting on the sofa, and Bogie was standing near the TV. Ernest Hemingway was being interviewed. And Bogie pointed at the TV and he turned to me and he said, Betty, that right there, that's the real shit."

I nod. I may say something about the writing, those early stories that everyone agrees were the real shit. Though I wouldn't have said *the real shit* back at her. Eventually they call for first team, Bacall nodding at me then exiting so we can shoot the scene where Christopher knocks her down while swiping the luxury lounge swag she's just scored. She surprises everyone with her willingness to stretch out on the cold ground for as long as we need to shoot the scene after the stunt double takes the fall for her.

Matt, an LA native, serves as culinary guide during the group's dinners out, his favorites in the family and Hollywood classics vein, with cocktails at Trader Vic's, an old-school Mexican meal in, I think, Marina del Rey, and a traditional American place somewhere mid-city providing a California version of comfort food, mildly healthier and less carb-loaded than the East Coast equivalent, all ending with the customary game of credit card roulette, waiters again and again drafted to select a card from a folded-up napkin, mine coming up twice over the week's worth of dinners, the time evidently having come to even out my earlier luck, my enjoyment of the game shrinking as a result.

I do, however, enjoy the shoot days. I admire the West Coast crew, almost totally without New York surliness. They are efficient and mostly friendly, many having followed mothers and fathers into film trades, proud of their skill and confident in their city's centrality to moviemaking. I am at the monitors watching the action when I hear our DP Phil say, "That guy is amazing." He is talking about the Steadicam operator, who has executed a tricky move with the bulky, gyroscopically balanced device whose robotic-looking arm carries the camera, the whole gadget harnessed to his body, its self-leveling function smoothing out footsteps when the operator walks or runs. Phil's compliment is notable, as he started *The Sopranos* as an operator, a job he'd done for many years under the guidance of some great DPs. Though I don't have the visual sophistication to tell a perfectly acceptable operator from a standout, I know enough to remember it, and a couple of years later it comes to mind when I've moved up full-time and am on a movie that brings on board a Dutch DP whose work on a

stark and glinting Swedish horror movie has caught our director's eye but who has no knowledge of US crews. Both director
and DP instantly understand they've been given a gift when
they see this same operator at work on a complicated shot that
will give the film, *The Fighter*, its gracefully energetic opening. Whether or not they remember I was the one who sent
the operator their way matters less than that they have one less
thing to worry about and thus one less thing to expect me to
fix.

Tim walks the long blocks up the Avenue de l'Opéra toward
the InterContinental Hotel with his pants off. He's wearing
boxers. He's walking fast. There are five of us walking beside
him, taking stills and video. We have recently left a piano bar,
where we were drinking and listening to music. We're on our
biggest trip of the season, to Paris, for a story line involving
Carmela Soprano and her friend Rosalie, played by Sharon
Angela, and have taken the opportunity before shooting starts
to enjoy our off hours.

In the bar Tim dared the production designer to sing a song
at the piano, and when the designer demurred, Tim offered to
walk back to our hotel with his pants off if he did. The designer,
who rarely drinks, allows himself to both quickly swallow
the pro forma substance in front of him and to be persuaded.
The pianist agrees to the concept, the designer carries off the
song quite nicely, and now we are marching up the Avenue de
l'Opéra alongside our director, laughing and shouting like the
innocents abroad that we are.

Also along for the Paris scouting trip are our first AD
Michael and DP Phil. With Tim and Bob, the designer, they
make up my favorite team. Michael has been with us from
the start, a remarkably even-tempered and tantrum-free first
who I've bonded with over our complementary musical tastes,

having for years exchanged CDs we burn of favored artists one of us feels the other doesn't know well enough. He's at this moment apparently fully recovered from his treatments for pancreatic cancer that will flare up in a few weeks and prevent him from returning to Paris for our few days of shooting. After another recovery, the cancer will come back and, two years later, prove fatal, bringing us all together for a memorial at which his wife distributes CDs of tracks he treasured.

We're joined on some of the Paris scouts by David and his wife, and Ilene, and during shooting by Edie Falco and Sharon Angela, whose characters' desire to see Paris serves as David's excuse for this episode's partial focus on France. We film at the Musée de Cluny, an ancient Right Bank church, and, in the middle of the night, the only time permitted, on the Champs-

Élysées, starting our day at 3:00 AM and finishing at dawn with a Technocrane shot that rises up over a nearby market, some of us having by that time been awake twenty-four hours straight. We'd spent the hours preceding that odd call time following Tim's previous path through Parisian nightlife, first traced a few years back during a *Sex and the City* shoot, where he'd been introduced to owners of high-end bars and impossible-to-get-into clubs. One of our stops is at a Right Bank discotheque, where we are led by the manager to a prime table near the dance floor, comped a bottle of otherwise absurdly expensive vodka, and paired up with a group of aristocratic Mexican women on a shopping spree, their scary-sounding spouses back home. This moment continues with a late-night nosh at a café, and it is there that one of the Mexican women says to the group of us, with all the hauteur of her circle's chauffeur-driven, charity-congested, shopping-centric life, "You're circus people, you movie men. Circus people."

We stare at her. We can't really argue. I think of it now and then. It might come to mind when I've been away from home for a while, my wife visiting weekends, or when back home while unpacking the boxes with the road kit I've accumulated. Circus people. It was dismissive, I think, but, in its capturing of the transitory relationships we build and the temporary homes we make as we move around, it was profound, too, and however clichéd might be applied even to people who follow less picaresque paths. Universally, you might even say.

15

The Writing Life

This memoir stems from more than the simple desire to capitalize on the success of a show I happened upon in the random course of a typical roving film career. It also comes out of a passion for books and reading and its occasional corollary, the in-my-case chiefly unsuccessful but never totally forsaken notion of being a writer. At its root are standard childhood traumas, my family's version starting with the then mysterious split of parents who never noticeably fought and rarely raised their voices – *Your father is moving closer to the office* was the sole explanation my mother offered me and my sister, aged ten and seven – and proceeding along common lines, resulting in enough disturbance to drive me to shoplifting, cigarette smoking, and other minor aggressions. The discovery in middle school of books resulted in a more reliable form of oblivion, and when the pull of the headier side of science fiction (Heinlein, Ellison) and the then faddish Hermann Hesse's thin and overwrought studies of young male sensibility waned, I left my room and went down to the living-room bookshelves where four stacked stretches of the Modern Library sat along with John O'Hara's *Appointment in Samarra* and Mario Puzo's *The Godfather*. Those two novelists' smoothly strung-together sentences and sexed-up subjects emboldened me to make the leap to the Sinclair Lewis volumes in their vicinity, then a shelf up into Dostoyevsky and thus into a whole other realm of ideas and emotions, carrying me out of my stifling suburban existence for hours a day for the balance of my middle and high school years.

Sometime a year or two into this spree I conceived the notion of pursuing as my livelihood what had helped me find a pathway out of dumb confusion. That this didn't in the end work out, beyond thirty-plus years of scattershot book reviewing, has left me grateful nonetheless for a life spent making as much time for literature as a time-devouring career has allowed. The early urgent reliance on books has kept me reading seriously and serially, and thinking periodically about literature while involving me in a couple of lifelong friendships and these, in conjunction with the reviewing, have given me a connection however tenuous to a life I haven't lived.

The first of these friendships started about when books become a big part of my life, though on meeting, neither of us, I think I can safely say, had a literary life in mind, our connection coming about simply because we were in the same class and played the same sports. Still, the unusual perceptiveness and empathy this friend soon manifested might as well be seen as foreshadowing his future vocation in poetry, most clearly exemplified for me during a game of H-O-R-S-E we were playing one day in his driveway. As this newish friend looked up at the garage-mounted backboard, dribbling before a shot, he talked about how he sometimes played this very game with his father when he came home from work, suddenly holding up on his shot and lowering the ball to a hip and saying something along the lines of, "Maybe it's hard for you to hear because your father's not around to do this kind of thing?" I was suddenly choked up and speechless, too startled by the question and too confused about the feelings it evoked to be grateful or to take advantage of a rare opening to talk about my relatively recently wrecked family, though I would come to think of that moment with wonder. How did a kid that age put himself in a place fully foreign to him and think to say something out loud about it?

This is Peter Cole. We will stay in touch from the time we leave Wayne, New Jersey, with an early period of relentless correspondence followed by a fallow couple of years that has since settled into periodic socializing and my fortunate and prized inclusion in Peter's readings and in his mailings of author's copies of his books, beginning with the publication in 1989 of *Rift*, with its fierce and difficult title poem, followed over the years (to date) by four more volumes of poetry, one of collected poems, numerous translations from Arabic and Hebrew, an anthology or two, and a number of slim, handsome novels written by Middle Eastern writers that he, his wife Adina Hoffman, and a friend select, edit, and publish in Israel, where Pete has lived on and off forever. Adina, also a writer, includes me in her writing life, too, occasionally sending a manuscript my way for thoughts, one recent one her concisely amusing and informative biography of screenwriter Ben Hecht. I don't help either of them with their writing, but their inclusiveness lends a sense of belonging, and I enjoy watching a childhood friend, against whom I batted in Little League and caught passes from in freshman football, publish books, show up in one of those *Paris Review* interviews, and collect a genius award from the MacArthur Foundation. I also catch him a few times as he works the worldwide literary festival circuit alongside the Palestinian poet Taha Mohammed Ali, whom he translates and for whom he and Adina become a two-person flack team, Pete and Taha's readings a kind of burlesque act, Taha reciting in Arabic and Pete in his English translations the poet's droll, accessible, scathing, punchy work, a mash-up of classic Middle Eastern imagery and allusions to Disney cartoon characters. Adina writes a poignant historical biography of the poet, delving into a life during which Taha ran a tourist trinket shop in Nazareth.

Post-college in New York, Pete generously introduces me to literary friends met while at Hampshire College. Among them is a poet who works as John Ashbery's amanuensis, a fiction writer in the CCNY MFA program, and Eli Gottlieb, whose 110th Street studio becomes the venue for a self-run writing workshop. Eli, who occasioned Barry Sonnenfeld's attack on the word *somnolent*, becomes my other enduring link to the writing life. A fiction writer who a decade and a half after we meet publishes a first novel and produces them periodically thereafter, his oeuvre alive with lovely language and a literary backbone that never allows its occasional genre encroachments to lower the prose into standard feints and expected resolutions, Eli too shares early versions of his work with me and unlike with Pete's poetry I feel more in my element and freer with suggestions, whatever help they end up being. I am also able at Eli's invitation over the years to meet working writers, agents, and editors, and to get astute early guidance for whatever writing I am managing myself.

His first novel, *The Boy Who Went Away*, leads to his winning a Rome Prize Fellowship in 1997 where, as previously mentioned, he remains for many years, renting a Trastevere apartment after his year at the American Academy. Tana and I visit him there the summer before 9/11, Jack in summer camp and *The Sopranos* on hiatus. As we drink and snack and catch up, Eli's local acquaintances roll in, among them Rocco Carbone, an amicably bibulous Italian novelist whom I first met when Eli lived in Padova in the late 1980s. I was spending a few months in France at the time, in emulation of all the writers who'd gone there. At that first encounter Rocco, ribald and provocative, poured out post-prandial grappa after grappa that cured me permanently of a taste for it. Years later I will spend time with him in New York, and not long after that Eli tells me he has died in a moto-scooter crash in Rome, not uncommon, evidently. Eli himself in his Roman years does a skin-flaying skid on a scooter, landing him in the hospital. Along with Rocco at that 2001 Roman dinner are the novelist and former Sontag secretary Sigrid Nunez, the poet Sarah Arvio, and Eli's cookbook-writing girlfriend. In later years I'll sit at tables or stand around at gatherings Eli arranges with Francine Prose, Walter Kirn, Mark Strand, Nick Flynn, and Phillip Lopate, grateful of inclusion, sometimes able to contribute showbiz gossip and behind-the-scenes anecdotes, and more starstruck myself than when in the presence of movie stars.

It is Pete, though, who arranges my first-ever literary encounter, which occurs during our freshman year at college on a trip to Boston in 1975 after I've announced my intention to be a writer but before, if I recall correctly, Pete has turned to poetry. With characteristic generosity he thinks that I'll be interested in meeting through family connections a young writer who recently published his first short story in *The Atlantic Monthly*, a first novel soon to come. In a neatly kept tenement apartment in East Boston with bookshelves the writer has built himself and a self-painted representation of a rooster or some similar animal over the fireplace, Pete and I introduce ourselves to John Sayles and his partner, Maggie Renzi. We talk books and writing for a while and then watch Maggie and John gather the neat stacks of spare change on their dining-room table and go with them to a farmers market.

A couple of years ago I round out that visit with a follow-up, Pete and Adina arranging a dinner at their part-time New Haven home, a reunion of fitting consequence only for me, as Pete sees Sayles periodically. I reviewed his bulky 2011 novel, *A Moment in the Sun*, my *Times Literary Supplement* editor having pushed it my way due to my overlapping interests in film and fiction. Before writing the review I caught up with a few of

John's books and a couple of movies, having fallen off an early fanaticism that had me rearranging bookstore shelves to turn copies of his first novel, *Pride of the Bimbos*, cover-forward as if the store had put it on special display, thrilled to watch someone I'd met rise into a writing career.

Ten years after that East Boston meeting I have published a few short stories in lit mags and taken the first step in what would prove to be the principal public aspect of my writing career by reviewing a short-story collection for a socialist monthly decades past its prime. *The New Leader* makes its home on Sixth Avenue and 28th Street in a building full of labor union offices and the medical providers and pension planners working with them, the garment industry location indicative of the journal's labor union roots and funding. Its print version will persist until 2006 and its online iteration until 2010, with Daniel Schorr the last boldface name in a chain that stretches back to Eugene V. Debs and includes Bertrand Russell, Ralph Ellison, Sidney Hook, and James Baldwin. I get my in when Tana designs a cover for them and mentions that her husband is interested in books and writing. Myron Kolatch, the editor, must at this point be consistently desperate for word count and instantly invites me in to browse the bookshelves and give it a try. I snag a Rick Bass story collection, my tastes at that point ruled by Gordon Lish, the influential and eventually somewhat infamous literary editor, one of whose Columbia University fiction workshops I've attended and who has mentioned Bass in typically praising/damning fashion, admiring the writing and commenting on the writer's short stature (Lish is not tall), using the phrase *little man* in one of the extended apostrophes that initiated his lengthy lessons. I get $50 from *The New Leader* for that inaugural piece. I would've done it for nothing. A few years later that's what I am getting, continuing to produce unpaid reviews for them for many years, my last on Thomas Pynchon's *Inherent Vice* in 2009.

Eventually I gather together some of these reviews and send them to fiction editor Lindsay Duguid at the *Times Literary Supplement* in London, which I read devotedly. Lindsay, as I come to address her in emails (we never meet, never speak on the phone), surprises me after long delay by assigning me a Sam Shepard story collection and shows me, in her deft and unobtrusive edits of that piece and dozens more over the next decade, how a talented editor can help sharpen language and clarify arguments, how guidance is better than fiat (at *The New Leader*, Myron would go years without touching much more than punctuation and then would rewrite and even insert sentences into articles in an undoubtedly well-meaning way, going to publication without telling me, illustrating for me more than a few times what the term *tin ear* might mean). I don't get to pick books at the *TLS*, don't in truth get any choice at all except to tell them now and then I don't have time due to film work, refusals I parcel out from fear of not being asked back. Lindsay once lets me know she won't be publishing my negative review of an unknown writer from a struggling press, opening my eyes to one more admirable quality an expert editor can manifest: mercy. She even publishes in the *TLS* a short and mostly positive review of an illustrated chapbook of my stories that appears as part of an arts project in 2007, and over the years assigns me a few page-long pieces that kick off the fiction section, the Sayles book mentioned earlier among them. The assignments thin out once Lindsay retires. Still, the long association with the *TLS* is a memorable one which, as an added benefit, brings me to the attention of editors at widely distributed, well-known US-based magazines and papers, *The Wall Street Journal* among them, who reach out to me and assign me articles. Once, my reviewing even garners me unheard-of name recognition when on putting my credit card down at the counter of a bookstore in Manhattan a clerk asks if I am the same person who writes for the *Times Literary Supplement*.

The move to Montclair and our son's attendance at its public grammar, middle, and high schools widen our circle of friends. The town's combination of proximity to the city (with ever imminent plans for a direct rail connection to Penn Station), distinctive prewar housing stock (as opposed to the viral replication of characterless suburban models in towns like Wayne where I grew up), and a few charming business districts with shops and restaurants and even an art-house movie theater, make it attractive to urban baby boomers with babies of their own. Those city types like hearing the town referred to as Park Slope West. Tana with her contrarian streak proudly tells people that we live in New Jersey, each time evoking from me the amendment, Montclair, hoping they've heard that the town is more than simply another dull suburb. Our cooking group (the town is also rife with type-A types whose jobs and kids aren't enough, stuffing their calendars with book- and cooking- and sports-related monthly meetups) includes a framer for art stars with a house full of unattainable treasures gifted to him from his clients; an artist with a New York gallery whose openings we happily attend every year or two and whose large-scale square canvases of dreamlike figures floating in colorful abstract backgrounds are mysteriously impactful; and a publishing exec and author who cooks fantastically complex and ambitious dishes as delicious as they are guilt-inducing given the obvious hours they require. We also cross paths periodically with a couple whose son is a close friend of our son's, the wife a writer for *The Washington Post* and the husband for *The New York Times*.

When the husband, who interviews me for a column in the metro section of the *Times*, hears that the part-time complement to my slot at *The Sopranos* is a regular *TLS*-reviewing gig, he offers to put me in touch with one of the Sunday *New York Times Book Review*'s editors.

Thus, Dwight Garner, having read through a handful of my *TLS* clippings, begins periodically to assign me pieces for the *Book Review* until he moves on to daily reviewing himself and his boss moves on, too. Dwight is another truly fine editor under whose aegis over three or four years I log a batch of reviews. Among these are – at least to me and at the risk of bragging (which I realize here and in what follows I am doing, but then that tends to happen when your underlying thought is you wish you had more than you do to brag about) – a few tangible literary milestones. I am among the earliest American reviewers to praise Roberto Bolaño and Ali Smith in in-brief reviews, having been assigned Bolaño's short novel *By Night in Chile*, his first to appear in English, and Smith's early collection *The Whole Story and Other Stories*. I also get a few flattering notes from Dwight that I prize and have clung to ever since, including praise relayed from editor in chief Sam Tanenhaus in response to an omnibus review I turn in for a page the *Book Review* is then experimenting with, the full text of which reads as follows:

> BTW, Sam T. thinks you are god; loved the first-novel piece, thought it a model of the genre.
> He has made this point now about 7 times.

At the peak of this period, Dwight flatteringly inquires about my interest in replacing a longtime *Book Review* weekly columnist. By doing quick math as to the hours I'd need to put in and the compensation on offer, I figure it will take me fifty hours a week to read and write about the required books for about one-tenth the money I earn in locations, which speaks to me of the financial rewards of the writing life.

My time at the *Times* comes with the occasional opportunity for conversational bragging, which I indulge when openings allow, thus giving rise to one uncomfortable moment that occurs in my father's basement when, during his regular end-of-year Christmas party, while I'm talking about recent assignments with his sister-in-law Clare, at that time head of Penguin, my dismissive description of one book I've just turned in a review of causes Clare to say, "Oh, Markie, you didn't pan that book?"

"I kind of did," I say.

"I paid a million dollars for it," she says.

I have no response. Clare doesn't wait for one. She walks away, heads up the basement stairs, and doesn't speak to me again that long Christmas Day, keeping her distance for I don't remember how many family gatherings after that.

16

Between Seasons: One Step Forward

For the first time in years there is only a few months' break between *Sopranos* seasons. Technically, the break is between season six, part one, which featured twelve episodes, and season six, part two, featuring nine, which as a practical matter is the show's seventh and final season. I have been turning down location work without having moved beyond it, but with the short break and *Sopranos* production to start up soon and to continue for a while – episodes now routinely take fifteen or so days so the nine that will finish off the show will take many months to film – I'm willing to wait, writing the book reviews that come along, beginning research for a piece on Tom McGuane I have proposed to editor Heidi Julavits at *The Believer*, for whom I've already written a couple of essays, and employing my limited home improvement skills around the house when tasks fall within range. And on the often imperfect parenting side, I act as coach for my son's indoor winter lacrosse team, bringing to the role inexperience and blood-based overenthusiasm. Jack has without our influence absorbed an interest in the game due to a long-standing local tradition of excellence in it. Early in the season I get tossed out of a game by the head referee for an act of sarcasm, to my wife's horror and the amusement of the other parents, who observe my walk across the playing surface (the only way out of the coaching box) and up into the stands, where I join them to shakes of head or pats on the back, after which I attempt to contain myself. Over the years I see myself far more easily roused to anger and spite than is seemly and am sometimes shocked by my vehemence and desire for vengeance after opposing goals or penalties.

I am barely settled into my post-season time off when *The Sopranos* UPM, who was most generous with advice when I first moved up, calls to ask if I want to take over a job he's been prepping but now can't cover, having found a more profitable way to spend his break. It's the Steve Buscemi movie *Interview* gone over earlier, its relatively tranquil shoot and pleasing result making tangible to me the notion that I might not stay in locations forever.

A second line producing job that, in conjunction with *Interview*, bookends the final season of *The Sopranos* will result in my not being on location when the finale is shot. This one shows me how disastrously wrong a production can go – long hours, low pay, fishy financiers who for weeks are late paying the crew and then finally fully fail to get a deposit to the bank, leading the crew to revolt. This happens on a Friday night a few weeks in, the department heads having come to me at call time to tell me that if their paychecks haven't showed up by the time lunch is called they are going home. The paychecks don't arrive, and after some loud and harsh commentary directed my way, the crew leaves. Soon after, I find out an electrician has swiped pricey lighting equipment and a production assistant has gone home with petty cash meant to come to set to reimburse others, holding the cash as ransom. When back pay and finishing money is finally furnished after a few down days, the petty cash gets restored, most of the equipment reappears, and we get through it. Half a year later my wife and I view the film in Philadelphia, where the story is set and was shot, at an event attended by the director and most of the cast. The crowd is kind, for a while, but soon the groans and laughter – there was nothing funny in the script – begin, and then the walk-outs commence. I feel badly for the director, a well-meaning man with a typical if mildly autocratic mien, and worse for the sincere, devoted, kindly cast, whose performances come across as either misguided or outlandishly over-the-top, the images up on the screen looking underlit at night and blandly bright by day, the mildly nonsensical script approaching incoherency in its underwhelming execution. But the fact is Hollywood, whether in low-, medium-, or high-budget mode, makes mostly lousy films, clichéd and sanitized, some of these unfortunately grandly financially successful and encouraging of more of the same. What can we who work in it say? It's a living. The Philadelphia film is not the first or last disaster I participate in and by doing so am at least partially responsible for, but at least it gets me one step further removed from locations and out of *The Sopranos* before the final episode starts shooting. David is directing, and everyone is avid for inclusion in the series' swan song. I'm no exception, but I realize I have no shot at anything approaching involvement in the implementation of whatever David has in mind, as there's a quartet of producers and UPMs above me, all scrambling to share their input, and a couple of other AUPMs around ready to plug any production holes that open up. I'm fine skipping the shoot, unaware that what's waiting for me in Philly is going to go so badly and turn into such a dud of a movie. In any case, it's another class in my producing education.

17

The Theater

John, the person I suggested my father reach out to when his wife, Grace, called to tell me he couldn't get out of bed, says the show is part of TV history and to the extent that I was part of it, I am, too. I'm not sure what occasions this moment of congratulatory reflection. My work on the show is done, the last season has aired, John is living in LA, his marriage to Grace's older sister Clare long over, and we are talking on the phone about what is in our respective entertainment-related futures, making it sometime between June 2007, when the last *Sopranos* episode aired, and 2010, when John dies. He always said he didn't expect a long life because his father died young, and he turns out to be correct, though whether what killed John has anything to do with his father is unclear. I always got the sense that he looked at his fate as justification for living it up, and that he did. He liked to drink. He went through a cocaine phase or two or three, as did most people working in these fields in the 1970s and 1980s. He tried, I know firsthand and from stories he told me, more than a few of the other substances passed around the arts scene in those years.

John grew up in Wayne, New Jersey, like me. He went to NYU to study acting, and graduated (I assume) more or less straight into André Gregory's Manhattan Project, a theater group formed in 1968 and acclaimed for a series of Off-Broadway experiments including a frantic staging of *Alice in Wonderland* that opened in 1970 and that my sister and I saw in an early iteration (I was twelve, Caroline nine), entranced by its energy and sexualized staging, and aware that the crowded, converted commercial space it took place in had nothing to do with what we up to then thought of as a theater.

John was dark-haired, swarthy, athletic in the way of some theater types: graceful with a slope-shouldered, smooth, cat-like physicality, as a performer good at playing sidekicks and jesters, roles he took on for the Manhattan Project and in productions at the Public Theater and its Shakespeare in the Park summer residences. We saw him in the striking 1978 mounting of *The Taming of the Shrew* starring Meryl Streep and Raul Julia, the latter of whom John became good pals with, Raul and John making trips out to New Jersey to meet up with my father at his club for tennis games, one time all of us driving back to the city together toward a Chinatown dinner (my father loved to arrange big gatherings at these basement spots, cart in a couple of magnum bottles of Italian wine, and pick up the tabs for everyone). I remember John talking enthusiastically about his friend, about the long unwinding he went through after playing the Shakespearean roles he took on, fired up and unable to sleep after performances. "And you should see what knocks on his hotel-room door," I recall John saying, full of admiration for his friend's substantial female fan base.

John is always upbeat, enthusiastic, a rallying force and supporter of everyone's best efforts. It is why I thought of him when my father hit his low point. My sister and I, on trips into the city with our father and his wife, had spent many hours with John and his troupe at Phebe's in the East Village, the gang streaming in post-performance to order rounds of drinks and burgers and fries, whooping it up like some idealized enactment of life in the theater, the director Wilford Leach often there, and always Larry Pine, Angela Pietropinto, and Tom Costello, fellow founding Manhattan Project members, and soon enough Wallace Shawn, with that squinching voice and cackle and unabashedly intellectualizing lexicon. John's wife would be present, too, always a good sport, equipped with ready sarcasm when called for and well respected by the group for her intelligence and self-possession. She would soon get a degree at a state school in north Jersey, start working as an editorial assistant at a publishing house, and in no time begin her ascent to the very top of a couple of major publishers, with roles as editor in chief and president, with bestselling authors as her friends and actors and politicians in her confidence. John seemed to regard her ultimate achievement as exactly proper and fitting, as he did with what he saw of mine, happy to award me my small place in TV history and always openly happy for me as I moved into production managing and producing roles on movies that made money or garnered awards.

Long before that he welcomed me into his world, bringing me along early in his push into directing. I'd moved to New York post-college the year he directed one of his first shows, Wallace Shawn's massive *The Hotel Play*, with its seventy-plus speaking roles. He let me sit in on rehearsals at La Ma Ma, where it would soon run, and we'd proceed from rehearsals to Phebe's, where I'd meet a cast culled from the New York world of arts well beyond acting, including *New Yorker* cartoonist Frank Modell (elderly, wry, stately), playwrights Ed Bullins, Christopher Durang, and Wendy Wasserstein (no memory), and fiction writer Ann Beattie (whose reply to my no doubt gushing praise was a sung "Ta-Ta-Ta-Da").

A year or so before *The Hotel Play*, I had sent John a one-act I wrote that earned me a co-share of my college's playwriting award, and after he got his first taste of directing, he had me get him a fresh copy, and then at a bar or burger joint or maybe walking down the street he told me it still read well.

"I'm gonna get it up on its feet," he said. "I'm gonna shoot it as a TV half hour and see if PBS or someone'll get interested."

He convinced Griffin Dunne, *The Hotel Play*'s star, to play the lead. I sat with John and Dunne in a diner to listen to John go over his plans, no memory of what was said but a very clear picture of Dunne's crush-inducing girlfriend Brooke Adams approaching the table at the end of our meeting and standing there, eyes for him only.

The play was unsubtly called *The Absent Father*. It swapped my solidly suburban home for Sam-Shepard-slanted blue-collar digs, keeping my frozen family life in place. John gathered cash from a theater investor, a small beat-up downtown video studio was secured, carpenters who built sets at the Public were borrowed to slam together a three-wall set, and I got to watch Dunne enact a sexed-up, dumbed-down version of me, Frank Modell making an appearance as my fictionalized grandfather, and Carrick Glenn playing whatever fantasy I had dreamed up for my character's partner. A few other Manhattan Project regulars strolled in and out. I think Angela Pietropinto played the mother. The dress rehearsal was laid down on tape and went no further. John moved on to directing Off-Broadway, took over a Broadway show from Leach (*Pirates of Penzance*, with Treat Williams), jumped into kids' TV, had a nice success directing stage and filmed versions of a one-woman show for the performance artist Reno, and then skipped out of his marriage and out of New York, landing for his last years in LA, where he continued to direct. I'd talk to him now and then. I'd run into his former colleagues on movie shoots. I remember having a long conversation with Michael Moran on the set of *Sleepers*. He was playing a judge. Large, boisterous, blunt, and kind, Mike had been a playwright when I first met him, the Manhattan Project staging one of his shows at the Public. He'd built sets, acted, done some directing, and no doubt ticked every other theater-worker box. He'd lived around the corner from John and Clare, longtime East Villagers, until Clare started to make real money and they bought something in the West Village. Mike had been at plenty of those nights at Phebe's. I was surprised he remembered me. I figured I'd blended into whatever background surrounded the troupe. He talked fondly of John's many indulgences and enthusiasms, for drugs and tennis and booze and food. Then he segued to John's recent tossing in the trash of a perfect marriage to a wife at the top of the world. I knew all about it. My father told me he and Grace had walked into one of their regular Chinatown places to spot John at a table with an attractive young woman, the raging inappropriateness of the picture they made matched by the enormous stupidity of the choice of venue, all of that trampled to insignificance by the fumblingly desperate excuse he lobbed at his brother- and sister-in-law, something about posters and concepts. If she didn't already know it, his wife soon found out what was up and that was that.

My father didn't lose touch with John. He'd report back when they talked. He'd tell me when John was coming east and they were getting together. I always thought John was good for him, John's enthusiasms and excesses an argument against the locked-in parts of my father, an invitation to talk about things he didn't normally talk about. I didn't think his golf friends' chatter went much beyond work and sports and . . . golf. I wondered if when he was bedridden and in the throes of collapse he had taken my suggestion and given John a call. I like to think he had, and that it helped, and that therefore both John and I had a hand in his recovery, which was swift and from what I saw enduring. When John died, I not only felt the loss of someone who'd been kind to me as a kid and welcoming to me as I took stabs at a career akin to his, but also knew I'd lost a purely positive link to my father, a direct connection to our earliest escapes from an otherwise fraught and fragmented family life when we would go to see John's plays and look on in joy and wonder at people who seemed to be exactly where they wanted to be, up on stage, making a living pretending to be things they were not.

18

My *Sopranos* Years, Part Six

The trips out of town again provide the most memorable moments for me during the shooting of *The Sopranos* final nine episodes. One early one finds us upstate scouting for the lake house where Tony takes his wife, Carmela; sister Janice (played by Aida Turturro); and her husband, Bobby (Steve Schirripa) to lay low for a while. We choose a place an hour and a half north of the city, close enough to bring people and equipment in and out on the same day even though the drive time means putting the core shooting crew and principal cast in a hotel. Tim, arguably the best action director in the stable, makes the most of the hand-to-hand battle between Jim and Steve, the two large men or their doubles effectively crashing around the lake house's living room, breaking multiples of the lamps and coffee tables that props and set dressing have lined up for the many takes we'll do, with Edie and Aida shouting in horror or glee on the periphery. Schirripa, whose character first showed up in the second season and who has grown into a key figure for the final few, has always delivered his lines in an aggrieved monotone that has a strange magic, another of the series' many actors of limited range used to perfection, anchored in the show's verisimilitude thanks to the endlessly evocative naturalism of its stars.

While staying upstate the cast and crew get together at the hotel bar every night after wrap, where a costumer shows amazing karaoke chops and where one night Jim stands beside location assistant Josh and me, the three of us running through that early-day internet-originated pastime of recalling silly-sounding sexual nomenclature and then providing their unthinkably intricate anatomical iterations (I recall Jim coming out with *pink sock*, one I haven't until that moment heard). When we notice Josh exchanging looks with one of the bartenders, Jim expands on the topic by asking him to tell us what he'd do to her if given the chance, and Josh, wanting to provide Jim with a bit of entertainment, goes at length into extremely stark sexual choreography. After this elaborate effort, he glances down at his phone to realize he has either pocket-dialed or not hung up on his girlfriend, who works on the show, too, but is not up north with us. He says, "Oh shit," takes his phone, and walks out of the bar, coming back later to inform us he no longer has a girlfriend, though I hear a few days later he has smoothed his way back into the relationship.

When David awards one of the directors of photography, Phil, a season six episode to direct, the couple of other crew members who have been angling for a slot (the other DP, the script supervisor) express their annoyance out loud. When someone asks Phil during a director's scout how it happened, he says simply, "I asked."

And why not? DPs along with first ADs and actors make good candidates for TV directing, where the vision and story sense are the province of showrunners and their writing staff and what's needed on set is an ability to judge performance, understand coverage, and keep things moving. Completing each day's work is the first hurdle for any episodic director. Capturing a convincing display of emotion in a sufficient selection of medium and close shots so that the showrunner has choices in the edit room, along with not antagonizing key people on the production, will get you hired back. A bit of flair might bring you to the notice of other showrunners and get you hired elsewhere. Phil is not only technically adept but intellectually sharp. He'll move out from behind the camera entirely and have a successful career in the directing chair not long after the end of *The Sopranos*.

His episode features another distant location, this one Miami, where the writers introduce a Cuban car-theft connection and Tony exercises his doubts about old-school associate Paulie Walnuts. For the culmination of that story line the script calls for us to get the actors and camera on a boat and bring it into heavy chop and out of sight of land. We do the usual scouting trip, come back home to finish prep, shoot out New York first – Lin-Manuel Miranda makes an appearance as a bellhop with a single scoffing line to Tony and Paulie – and then get back on airplanes in early December to film our four days in Florida, cast-wise bringing Jim, Tony Sirico, and semi-regular Paulie Herman, playing the crippled Beansie and valued among the cast and crew for his role as maître d' at one of the more popular restaurants in LA.

Boat work is always tight, and there is no room for me on the one we're shooting, so for no good reason I ride along with the Miami-Dade County marine police in a freakishly fast boat that seems to skim across the tops of the three-foot waves we are working in. The police race around to chase away the occasional onlooker but mostly do nothing and three or so hours later lead the way back to the South Beach marina we started from. Once docked we film belowdeck scenes, simulating rough seas by having a couple of prop people hand-rock the boat, the camera operator tilting the camera side to side to add to the illusion.

After the last night of filming, we follow a few of the locals to a restaurant near our Hollywood, Florida, hotel, where we eat seafood and drink lots. I am back in my hotel room when someone calls or texts me to join the reconstituted festivities at the hotel's outdoor pool. Even before I look over the railing of the narrow balcony of my room I hear shouts, laughter, splashing. There are a dozen people down there. I put on a suit and head down.

Minutes later I'm in the water and Jim hands me a bottle of cognac, from which he's been drinking. It's approaching midnight. I'm happy. I don't usually take the opportunity to get involved in Jim's after-hours activities. I admire his acting, like everyone else, and as I get to know him a little, I find I like him, too, his shyness and sensitivity and easy humor. I also understand the appeal of the crew members he's fallen in with, entertaining, loyal, up-for-anything types. But none of them have made this trip. Filling in are those of us still awake, Phil, the camera operator bumped up to be his DP, our gaffer, a couple of others. Some of the locals from the dinner join in. One is a local PA who's in the pool taking slugs from the bottle, too. At some point the hotel manager comes out and tells us apologetically that there have been complaints and we have to wrap it up. Just before this happens someone has made a run, there's a cooler full of beer, and everyone wants to keep going, and since there's a beach a hundred yards away, that's where we head. We sit in the sand with beers, the dark skittering edge of the waves just visible in front of us, when Jim suggests a night swim. I instantly go into worst-case-scenario mode, imagining him or someone swallowed up by the ocean. I understand what it will mean to have been the production person not only assigned to this unit but also present for and participating in the disaster.

"I don't think it's a good idea," I say.

I am standing up. They're all sitting in the sand in front of me. Seven or eight people. I have had just enough to drink to be loud enough to get myself heard over the waves. Later, after everyone but me has taken their dip, Jim invites us up to his room, a suite on an upper floor, where I see more peril – thin balconies with low rails – and where Jim announces he wants to take a shower to warm up and anyone is welcome, and that local PA is instantly up for it, and in a short time Jim is there in the shower in his bathing suit with this woman about half his size and a couple of people standing around in the large-ish bathroom laughing and drinking, one leaning into the hot water to splash the chill off as I pause at the bathroom door before heading out of the room, into the hallway, into the elevator, and into my room, the next morning climbing into the van to the airport to catch the flight home.

On the beach, though, to backtrack, when I'm repeating to the group that I don't think swimming is a good idea, everyone now up and starting to walk down to the water, Jim looks at me and says, "Why not?"

"The waves sound pretty big," I say. "I mean, there might be a rip current or something."

He nods, one of those smirking, evaluative looks on his face, and moves past me. They all continue toward the water. I do, too, as far as the foam. Jim looks back at me before running in.

"What," he says to me, "you're gonna save me, Mark?"

We are invited to the funeral, the cast and crew, and most of us go. It's a sticky and still day, June 27, 2013, half a dozen years after the finale has been filmed, everyone involved dispersed into the rest of our lives. Jim died of a heart attack in Rome four days earlier. The ceremony is held at the enormous and never-quite-finished Cathedral of St. John the Divine on the Upper West Side. The place is packed. We see hundreds of people we know, *Sopranos* cast and crew and others who have worked with Jim more recently. I'll hear Terry Winter talk in a radio interview about the shock he felt on hearing the news, and I'll hear David say later that unlike Terry, he has been expecting this call for years. He means, I take it, that Jim's overindulgence and bingeing wildness, weight gain and lack of care taken with himself could lead only to this, an early death. As usual, it's hard to argue with David's way of seeing things.

19

Breaking the Fourth Wall

David asks me to read a three-part series he's written two scripts for, with the third by sometime *Sopranos* writer Lawrence Konner and a partner. HBO has told David it will be made if the price comes down, the goal to hit something like a $60 million all-in budget, and he's thinking he could work with me on it. By now I've been line producing for a while, but the idea of filling that role on a project by David feels like something of an arrival.

I like David's scripts a lot, the third less, and give him my thoughts on how to hit the number and, because he asks, what I think of the scripts, his two presenting a rich, gritty account of Hollywood history by following fictional characters through the decades, the final one offering up a less aggressive look at our era and placing a prominent real-life star into the action as a central character. We exchange a few more calls and I have a couple with HBO, at which point we all realize the project is not getting greenlit anytime soon. The calls soon cease, and I move on to whatever is next for me.

A few years later, in early 2018, David reaches out again, this time about a Sopranos prequel, and after reading that script I meet him at the Hôtel Plaza Athénée, not far from his New York apartment. Again, he seems interested in hearing my thoughts about more than production elements. I greatly admire the script and tell him so (aware that all praise must hit him somewhat like it did Tony Soprano in the season five episode where Tony tunes in with paranoid intensity to the too-ready and raucous laughter of his subordinates after he has told an unfunny joke), expressing reservations only about the very Sopranos-appropriate racist punch line of the opening scene, worrying that a decade after the series has ended cultural sensitivities will make it more than a bit awkward given the current awareness of where racism leads, police shootings and protests all over the news. I worry aloud that placing the scene at the opening of the film and at such a remove from its episodic source will too quickly turn off too much of the audience.

"You think so?" he says in the even-toned way he has of letting you know you've been heard without revealing what he thinks about what you've said.

A week after our meeting, I write him an email about a riot sequence I've seen in the recent Kathryn Bigelow movie *Detroit* that might help with an approach to a similar scene in his script. My next correspondence about the project is to my agent, in March, after David has informed me he won't be directing. He tells me that two *Sopranos* directors (my favorites) have turned the movie down due either to lack of availability or for other reasons he doesn't divulge or I have since forgotten, though I do remember he seems disappointed.

In May a production executive at New Line gets in touch with and hires me to put together a schedule and budget, and I am paired with an accountant and we get to work. I send schedule drafts to David, standard procedure for me in these situations as I want to make sure the director or creative producer, if the director is not yet attached, is comfortable with the number of shooting days. Three months later, on June 5, I send an email to the New Line executive informing her that we have a New York budget, later that day send it over to her, and on June 7 bill for my work. In late June I meet with David, his wife, and an assistant at his Upper East Side apartment. I am brought to a small parlor or living room. I accept a glass of water, which a maid brings, and sit on a chair or sofa at some distance from everyone. It is not a warm or even comfortable environment, and David's gaze and inexpressive mien make me feel under a very distant and severe scrutiny, but as I am used both to David's affect and these kinds of pre-prep examinations, I don't feel particularly ill at ease. It is here I am informed who the director of the movie will be. Hearing the name, I'm half glad to be on the verge of starting a job, though I'm still hoping to do *The Sopranos* movie and tell David when the job I'm about to start will end.

I don't hear anything for a bit and am already in Philadelphia on the movie when David's assistant calls to set up a meeting with David and the new director. On July 18, I take the train to New York and make the ten-minute walk from Penn Station to HBO's East Coast base, where David keeps an office. I continue to feel an allegiance to the world of *The Sopranos* and to David. The script he and his partner have written is far better than the one for the job I'm on, better than that script will be even after it is torn apart and reconstructed, its scene order shuffled, its dialogue reconceived from scratch by a highly paid and touted Hollywood writer with input from two of Hollywood's most financially successful producer-directors and their in-house producers, our own director, an assortment of studio executives, our star, and his producing partner. We will eventually shoot the movie with a script that never fully makes sense, and the final product, even after an extensive reshoot, will continue to not fully make sense. The movie will fail to gather steam in the opinions of critics or in the public marketplace. The project is, however, a steady paycheck for its half year or so, and that's as much as I ever expect, and *The Sopranos* job is not quite real yet. Though there is now a director, there are no stars attached and no start date set.

———

Twice in my career I have commenced a meeting thinking we will be talking about how to approach a production only to realize I am being interviewed rather than consulted. In both instances, I do not respond well to this realization. The first time it happens, on a conference call, after starting to answer what I think of as a question oddly abstracted from the matter at hand, I say out loud something like, "Wait, is this an interview?"

In response the people interviewing me hesitate and hedge for a while before one of them tells me I should think of it as a sign-off rather than an interview, which to me sounds like another way of saying it is an interview, and that's what I say to them, and not in a delicate way. The call becomes acrimonious and ends a short time later. Interestingly, I do not lose the job, as the showrunner, with whom I've done three movies, wants me to produce his show and doesn't care that those he's hired ahead of me think my employment hinges on them.

In the meeting with David and the director of the nascent *Sopranos* movie, the realization that I'm being interviewed comes well into our conversation, after pleasantries are exchanged and the three of us catch up. We have already talked about a few recently released and grandly successful superhero movies, during which I have readily admitted to a distinct dislike of the genre, aware the director did one. David acknowledges that he, too, has no interest in them, though his dismissal is measured and brief, whereas I spend some time developing my thesis, shamelessly bringing up the article I recently wrote for the online *TLS* on the topic and repeating for the benefit of the room the torture I underwent forcing myself to sit through the dozen or so entries I endured.

As counterargument, the director asks me if there isn't some merit to the comic awareness and intellectual play certain of these movies employ, for example when the writers and directors break the fourth wall, letting the audience in on the fantastical assumptions being made. This leads to a discussion of the amusements to be had at movies like *Deadpool*, and I agree that the title sequence and the first half hour or so had freshness and wit before sliding into the typically plodding plot turns and overextended battle sequences that always leave me itching to exit the theater or turn off the television.

My surprise-interview alarm bell rings soon after this when the director asks me what I believe a line producer's function on a movie is. It is the same question someone asked me during the conference call mentioned above. I don't remember what I answer, but the realization of being mid-interview annoys me, and I'm not sure how well I hide that. The director then goes on to criticize the scenes I've chosen to show as day one in the schedule I've done, saying he'd never want to start off with such charged, performance-intensive material. I (defensively, I admit) explain that when I make a schedule it is done strictly to gather elements for budgeting, that I make sure the first AD in consultation with the director makes the schedule we will follow for filming and that I don't even show my schedule to the AD, who will inevitably do a far better job than me. The interview ends soon after this.

Late that day, having returned to Philadelphia, I send an email to the New Line executive informing her that I have met with the director and David and that I will be updating the schedule somewhat based on our discussions. Soon after that David calls to say they won't be moving forward with me. Given my behavior in the interview, I'm amazed I take this badly, but I do.

"The studio has someone they're more used to working with," he goes on to explain.

I am further upset that he is taking what I consider to be

an easy way out – blaming on the studio what is to me clearly a decision coming from him and the director, though in my mind it's the director who's ruled me out and David is simply performing his producorial duty.

"Yeah, right, David," I say.

It is as much of a protest as I can muster. It is enough. I hear both ire and disbelief in the way he mimics my words back at me when he says, "Yeah, right? That's what you're saying?"

The truth is, I don't know that the meeting meant anything. It's possible that the director, remembering me only as a location manager, had no intention of hiring me as a producer. I know that I wouldn't have hired me if I'd been the one doing the interviewing. In the end, I was more disappointed in the way the possibility of the job ended than in not doing the job itself.

Epilogue

A couple years after *The Sopranos* wrapped I was a full-fledged production manager making my first forays into producing movies with real budgets and stable financing. I was spending months at a time away from home. We soon sold our house and moved back to the city to make life more manageable. This way Tana could visit me on location when she wanted to without worrying about whether the basement would flood or the boiler would crap out. And she would no longer have to deal, when home alone, with a smoke alarm with a low battery chirping in the middle of the night or yet another creature finding a crack in from outside, another bat, for example, making its way down the chimney to fly circles around the downstairs rooms, this time with no lacrosse-playing son to net it and whisk it outside. In an apartment she could hit the light switch, lock the door, and let the superintendent deal with whatever went wrong. Jack, meanwhile, on graduating college would move back to New York and soon after take a job in Los Angeles, where he'd spend half a dozen years and give us an even better reason than my periodically necessary in-person appearances to spend time there.

I mostly steered clear of TV shows after *The Sopranos*, knowing that nothing was going to match what I'd spent all those years on and in my new role not really interested in the simultaneous prepping and shooting pace TV shows require, for line producers in particular a wrenching and in my experience unsatisfying way to be in this business.

One of my first big post-*Sopranos* jobs came when Jeff, the producer who'd bumped me up on the Wayne Kramer movie, brought me down to Philly with him to production manage the revenge flick *Law Abiding Citizen*, which resulted in a nine-month stint. Almost immediately following that we hooked up with David O. Russell for *The Fighter*.

That stellar film was in its making a model experience for me, compact and memorable, not easy by any means but carried out with a real team feeling, all of us living in an off-ramp Marriott Residence Inn near the town of Lowell, Massachusetts, where the film was set and almost entirely filmed, its rare triumphant rollout melding box office success, critical esteem and award attention. For the next few years I kept myself in production rhythm with David, fitting his next two similarly accomplished films, *Silver Linings Playbook* and *American Hustle*, in among an array of other projects that afforded me crash courses in visual effects and adult comedy (*Ted* and *Ted 2*) and the outfitting, fielding, and filming of period baseball teams surrounded by large crowds, one crucial location requiring the construction of hundreds of feet of telephone-pole-supported plywood walls painted green to ease the digital conversion of an unused minor-league ballpark in Chattanooga, Tennessee, in 2012, into Ebbets Field, Brooklyn, circa 1950 – this for the Jackie Robinson biopic *42*, at its center the brilliant, lovely, and too-soon-passed discovery, Chadwick Boseman.

In this way I pursued a typically peripatetic producing career around the country for the rest of the 2010s, picking my projects based on the people in charge – directors I liked or thought I would, creative producers with good reputations – or the scripts I was shown. When Covid hit and everyone in the film and every other business took a mandatory monthslong workplace hiatus, Tana and I settled uncomfortably into our apartment, donning masks for grocery runs and like everyone else wiping down or washing off what we brought back from our local stores' depleted shelves, and for exercise riding our bikes along eerily empty city streets to Central Park, horrified each time we did a lap around the park's perimeter by the freakish field hospital suddenly manifest in its northeast quadrant. Five months in, I got a call from a writer-director I'd done a movie with who'd been asked by HBO to come up with a Covid-friendly show. Thus began – after more calls, budget exercises, the online scouting of sites, some Zoom-room deal-making, and, most vitally, the expedited and supremely adept writing of a pilot and then five more follow-up scripts – the preparation for the first season of Mike White's *The White Lotus*, a show that would bring me back full circle, you could say, to the world of episodic TV at its best.

We're now two seasons in with a third on the way. The interest from family and friends in what's going on along with the constant public conversation and speculation about what it means and where it's headed feels familiar, but as I'm now seeing things from a producer's perspective, it's also all a bit new to me, too. The stresses of the job are similar, but the rewards – personal and public – are on a whole other level. I remain, nevertheless, well aware that while Mike is irreplaceable, there are others quite capable of doing what I do, while also feeling far more securely the centrality of my place on the show and the importance of the contributions I make. Naturally enough, given the sequel-centric business I'm in, I've started to think it, too, might someday be worth writing about.

Acknowledgments

I'm grateful to the people in the film business who hired me, instructed me, referred me to others, and promoted me, turning me from an underemployed thirty-something into someone with a health and pension plan and, not incidentally, a career. These included Ezra Swerdlow, Amy Herman, Bart Wenrich, Carol Cuddy, Ilene Landress, Neri Tannenbaum, and Jeff Waxman. Thanks in turn to the people I hired who made me look better at my job than I was and thus contributed to my continued employment and promotion.

Thanks to Eli Gottlieb, Peter Cole, and Adina Hoffman, who kept me in the loop of their writing lives, inspiring me to sit at my desk in off hours, on weekends, and when I was between film jobs.

On hearing I was working on this book, Jeanne Baer graciously introduced me to her former Norwich, Vermont, neighbor, Steerforth Press publisher Chip Fleischer. Chip took it on with inspiring enthusiasm and, as great editors do, made it better with a light touch and a great sense of sound and structure. And thanks to the rest of the Steerforth team, who have been terrific to work with: Anthony LaSasso, David Goldberg, Helga Schmidt, and Devin Wilkie.

And thanks again, and always, to my wife, Tana, whose belief in me through the years described in these pages and for all the years since has made it all possible.

READING GROUP GUIDE

1. Does *On Locations* make a career in film production sound like something you'd want? What would you enjoy doing? What would you find challenging or disagreeable?

2. The book opens with a chapter about Mark Kamine's father. What was the effect, in a book primarily about working in the film business, of starting with a personal story? Did it prepare you for what was to follow?

3. Among the stars, directors, writers, and showrunners, which of these "larger-than-life" people did you find most appealing? Which did you find least appealing? Which would you want to meet for coffee, and what questions would you ask if you did?

4. The "New Jersey Family" chapters include painful and embarrassing elements but also moments of understanding and reconciliation. Do you think Mark ended up in a good place? How do you think his upbringing and home life affected his work?

5. Mark relates acts of petty theft and dishonesty that he engaged in at the start of his film career, and in the "Crime Series" chapter he talks frankly about more lucrative scams that his superiors perpetrated. What does this tell you about the film business? Did you expect it? Do you think that kind of activity is likely more prevalent in the entertainment world than others?

6. Over the course of the six "*Sopranos* Years" chapters, the show and its cast go from anonymity to acclaim and fame. Were the effects of success on the people involved, on the way we look at TV series, and on the author what you expected?

7. In Mike White's foreword, he disagrees with Mark's observation in the second of the "*Sopranos* Years" sections that, beyond a small circle of key cast and creative leaders, everyone on a film shoot is replaceable. Who's right?

8. Did you like the way David Chase handled his showrunning duties on *The Sopranos*? Did the way he treated the writers he worked with make sense to you? What about the crew with whom he worked? What would you have done differently?

9. James Gandolfini, another central pillar of *The Sopranos* success, often shows great generosity and occasionally lapses into bad behavior. How did you feel about him at the end of *On Locations*? Did you appreciate his accomplishments as much as ever? Do you think actors' off-screen lives have any bearing on their work?

10. What other shows or movies would you welcome a behind-the-scenes look at? Are there particular aspects that went into the making of those shows you'd be curious to learn more about?

11. What effect do you think reading *On Locations* would have on someone interested in working in this field? If you had a friend or relative who wanted a career in film and TV, would you give them this book? Why or why not?

12. Does learning about what goes on behind the scenes deepen your understanding of some of your favorite movies or TV shows? Do you think you'll look at the next series or movie you watch differently?